The Genius of Impeachment

The Genius of Impeachment

The Founders' Cure for Royalism

John Nichols

THE NEW PRESS

NEW YORK
LONDON

Published in the United States by The New Press, New York, 2006
Distributed by W. W. Norton & Company, Inc., New York

ISBN-13: 978-1-59558-140-2 (pbk)
ISBN-10:   1-59558-140-5 (pbk)
CIP data available

The New Press was established in 1990 as a not-for-profit alternative to the large,
commercial publishing houses currently dominating the book publishing industry. The
New Press operates in the public interest rather than for private gain, and is committed
to publishing, in innovative ways, works of educational, cultural, and community value
that are often deemed insufficiently profitable.

www.thenewpress.com

Composition by dix!
This book was set in Bembo

Printed in the United States of America

10   9   8   7   6   5   4   3   2   1

CONTENTS

by GORE VIDAL

Of course George Bush and Dick Cheney have committed acts that would merit impeachment. In a proper country, they would be tried as traitors. You don't lie to a country, get it into a war, waste a trillion dollars, kill a lot of people all because of your vanity and lust for oil and admiration for your corporate partners. If that isn't treason, I don't know what is.

It is a crisis, but, after all, crises are supposed to be met bravely and surmounted by whatever means a democratic society would like to employ.

I suppose it might be simpler to add a Constitutional amendment creating the right of recall, so that the people, when they realize that the administration is insane, or totally corrupt, or is going to destroy the country through attacks on enemies that are no threat, may act to address the crisis. We know that, when they are aware of their authority, the people are more than willing to exercise it. I was in California when poor Gray Davis was being thrown out. Davis was a perfectly standard, ordinary, not-particularly-corrupt governor, but they got him out and they got the Terminator in. There was excitement, real excitement, at the thought that citizens could do something about an executive who had lost their approval—that they were, temporarily, in charge. If there was a right of recall at the federal level, I have no doubt that the movement to remove the president, the vice president and other members of the administration would be advancing with great strength and speed at this point.

We do not have recall at the federal level. But we do have impeachment.

What's in the Constitution is in the Constitution. We do not need the House or the Senate to vote on what the Constitution says. The Constitution says that a president, or a vice president, for that matter, shall be impeached for high crimes and misdemeanors. Well, we have seen the high crimes and misdemeanors. They are in evidence.

Impeachment is available to us as an option for addressing the crisis of George Bush's presidency. It can be done. The discussion is in the air, as it should be.

The moment has now grown dangerous, what with the president elevating himself to godhood, to a place so far above the law that he no longer can be bothered to acknowledge it. The very sight of the president signing, as his Constitutional duty, legislation out of Congress telling him "thou shalt not torture," and then saying that he does not feel bound by that legislation ought to seal the case—of course the president is bound by this legislation, and if he acts as if he is not bound by it you can impeach him. That's the original intent.

This president is so plainly guilty of so many things that he would be impeached by even a moderately impartial House, then tried and found guilty by a similarly impartial Senate. I don't see any problems or confusions there, except partisanship and a media which is vicious and which has already chosen sides and will smear anybody who tries to see that justice is done.

Americans have been hypnotized by the mantras that our would-be fascists keep chanting. "Inherent powers of the commander-in-chief in wartime"? Well, there is no war. No war has been declared. This is not wartime. The president does not have inherent powers of any sort; he has enumerated powers. The Constitution tells you exactly what they are, including the responsibilities of the commander-in-chief: to repel invasions and so forth. George Bush has so clearly exceeded his authority.

The people, I think, understand this. But, because our media has not informed them, and because our education system has not educated them, the people do not know what to do. I would advise them to read the Constitution. Read this history of impeachment. There is fodder here for patriots.

Henry B. González

*"We did not pledge an oath of allegiance
to the president but to the Constitution."*

HOMAGE TO HENRY B. GONZÁLEZ: AN INTRODUCTORY NOTE ON THE NECESSITY OF GETTING COMFORTABLE WITH IMPEACHMENT

I appeal to the future for my vindication.
Henry B. González

For the last quarter of the American century, the lonely task of maintaining the essential infrastructure of the American experiment—the system of checks and balances that George Washington identified as the nation's primary protection against the "love of power, and proneness to abuse it" that was certain to be entertained by the executives who succeeded him—fell to the son of Mexican-American immigrants who had been born Enrique Barbosa González in the barrio of San Antonio.

Henry B. González, as he was known during the thirty-seven years he served in the U.S. House of Representatives, learned his Constitution well at St. Mary's University School of Law in his family's adopted city. He adhered to the document's demands with a passion rarely mustered by members of Congress who could trace their bloodlines back to a revolution fought against the royal prerogative. Perhaps it was González's experience of battling the Texas segregationists of the 1950s—as a state senator who led the longest filibuster in the history of the Texas legislature to block bills written to circumvent the U.S. Supreme Court's *Brown v. Board of Education* decision—that inspired him to stand, often alone, in defense of the rule of law. Perhaps it was the experience of challenging the most powerful Anglo Democrats in Texas as the first serious Hispanic candidate for the governorship of that state, in 1958, that gave him the courage to raise a sometimes solo voice against presidents engaged in the "elected despotism" against which Jefferson had warned the protectors of the republic to maintain their guard.

"In terms of teaching Anglos that Mexican-Americans and other minorities are entitled to equality," the Lone Star State political seer Maury Maverick observed of González, "he was in Texas 50 percent Tom Paine, 50 percent Thomas Jefferson."

In Washington, González was 100 percent of what the founders intended a member of Congress to be.

Whatever the impetus for his intense adherence to the rules of the Republic, Henry B. took the long view of his membership in Congress. He was not merely there to represent the constituents back home in Bexar County, although his championship of their interests was legendary. And he was certainly not there to practice blind partisanship or ideological loyalty, although he was remembered by those who knew him as one of the truest and greatest progressives of the twentieth century. He was in Congress, González believed, to uphold an oath of office that committed him to "support and defend the Constitution of the United States against all enemies, foreign or domestic." And so he did, even when those enemies resided in the White House.

The congressman from Texas was sometimes jokingly referred to by colleagues as Henry B. González, D-Impeachment.

González proposed and supported more impeachments against more presidents than any member of the House in the history of the land.

He did so without fear of the political fire he would feel for counseling Congress to remove popular executives.

He did so without expectation of success in Congresses that showed little stomach for the work of checking and balancing presidents in the manner that the authors of the American experiment had intended.

He did so without concern for the fact that many of his articles of impeachment were penned in times of war and national uncertainty.

Indeed, it was precisely because the nation had been forced by illegitimate means into circumstances of war and turmoil that González believed he was required to act.

A supporter of moves to impeach Vice President Spiro Agnew and President Richard Nixon in the 1970s, González grew increasingly concerned during that decade by what he referred to as "presidential government," a catchphrase for concentration of federal government decision-making and power in the executive branch at the expense of the other branches of government.

To his view, "presidential government" was an affront to the Constitution that required a congressional challenge—up to and including impeachment of its practitioners.

It was in 1983 that González first stepped out on the limb of impeachment in a major way, joining seven other House Democrats—Ted Weiss of New York, John Conyers Jr. and George W. Crockett Jr. of Michigan, Julian C. Dixon and Mervyn M. Dymally of California, Gus Savage of Illinois, and Parren J. Mitchell of Maryland—in proposing H. Res. 370, "A resolution impeaching Ronald Reagan, President of the United States, of the high crime or misdemeanor of ordering the invasion of Grenada in violation of the Constitution of the United States, and other high crimes and misdemeanors ancillary thereto."

Attempting to impeach the popular Reagan was a lonely gesture that *Time* magazine correctly predicted would go nowhere. But it was hardly illegitimate. Though the United States faced no conceivable threat from Grenada, a tiny Caribbean nation, the entire population of which could fit into a professional football stadium, Reagan had ordered an invasion of the country without seeking a declaration of war or meeting any of the basic requirements of the Constitution with regard to warmaking. No less a commentator than John B. Oakes, the respected senior editor of the *New York Times,* would observe at the time that "President Reagan's consistent elevation of militarism over diplomacy creates a clear and present danger to the internal and external security of the United States. Presidents have been impeached for less."

Four years later, the elevation of militarism over diplomacy reached its peak with the revelation that the Reagan administration had engaged in the sale of arms to Iran, an avowed enemy of the United States, and had then used proceeds from those arms sales to illegally fund the Contras, a thuggish guerrilla group seeking to overthrow the left-wing government of Nicaragua. Again there was recognition on the part of serious observers of national affairs that it was entirely appropriate to raise the issue of impeachment. Veteran *New York Times* political writer Tom Wicker wrote in December of 1986 that "the offenses resulting from [Reagan's] policy, or his somnolence on the job, are more serious than any charge the House Judiciary Committee approved against Mr. Nixon." Two months later, *Times* columnist Anthony Lewis, who was broadly regarded as one of the nation's leading thinkers on constitutional matters, wrote: "In Watergate, the impeachment process carried forward so impressively by the House Judiciary Committee viewed the President's responsibility in constitutional terms. Each of the three articles of impeachment approved by the committee found, in different particulars, that President Nixon has violated the duty put on Presidents by the Constitution to take care that the laws be faithfully executed. The abuses of power now known to have taken place in the Reagan administration are more serious, more fundamental, than those involved in Watergate."

But, in Congress, there was a determination to avoid holding a president as popular as Reagan to account. Only one member rose to call for impeachment: Henry B. González.

On March 5, 1987, the day after Reagan acknowledged that the allegations against him were true—telling a national television audience that "a few months ago I told the American people I did not trade arms for hostages. My heart and my best intentions still tell me that's true, but the facts and the evidence tell me it is not"—the congressman from San Antonio proposed H. Res. 111. The resolution contained articles "[impeaching] Ronald W. Reagan, President of the United States, for high crimes and misdemeanors, including: (1) his approval and acquiescence in shipping arms from Israel to Iran; (2) his approval and acquiescence in covert actions conducted by the Central Intelligence Agency regarding the shipment of HAWK missiles to Iran; (3) his failure to notify Congress of continuing arms sales and covert actions; (4) his approval, acquiescence, or failure to prevent the diversion of proceeds from the Iran arms sale to the forces fighting the Government of Nicaragua; and (5) his disregard for the laws of the United States and pattern of casual and irresponsible decision-making."

González was without cosponsors. The Democrats who controlled Congress, with their eyes on what they thought was the certain prize of the presidency in 1988, chose not to impose the appropriate sanction on Reagan or Vice President George Herbert Walker Bush.

Four years later, when now-president Bush's approval rating soared to 91 percent after the launch of the Persian Gulf War, few Democrats in Congress were willing to note that the war had not been properly declared. And only one would state that the failure by the president to obtain that declaration required his impeachment: Henry B. González.

On the eve of the attack, the congressman had proposed H. Res. 34, which sought the impeachment of Bush for preparing to take the country to war without obtaining the consent of Congress. "When I took the oath of office earlier this month, as I had numerous times before, I swore to uphold the Constitution," González explained to his colleagues on January 16, 1991. "The president's oath was the same, to uphold the Constitution of the United States. We did not pledge an oath of allegiance to the president but to the Constitution, which is the highest law of the land. The Constitution provides for removal of the president when he has committed high crimes and misdemeanors, including violations of the principles of the Constitution. President Bush has violated these principles."

On February 21, 1991, at the very height of Bush's popularity, the congressman returned to the floor of the House to propose H. Res. 86, a measure prepared with the assistance of a brilliant professor of international law at the University of Illinois, Francis Boyle, which:

> [impeached] George Herbert Walker Bush, President of the United States, for high crimes and misdemeanors, including: (1) violating the equal protection clause of the Constitution by putting U.S. soldiers in the Middle East who are overwhelmingly poor white, black, and Mexican-American, as well as basing their military service on the coercion of a system that denies viable economic opportunities to these classes of citizens; (2) bribing, intimidating, and threatening others, including the members of the United Nations Security Council, to support belligerent acts against Iraq; (3) preparing, planning, and conspiring to engage in a massive war against Iraq employing methods of mass destruction that would result in the killing of tens of thousands of civilians, many of whom would be children; (4) committing the United States to acts of war without congressional consent and contrary to the United Nations Charter and international law; and (5) preparing, planning, and conspiring to commit crimes against the peace by leading the United States into aggressive war against Iraq in violation of the U.S. Constitution and certain international instruments and treaties.

González was particularly proud of the linkage that his articles of impeachment made between the costs of war to the national treasury and the cuts that would be made at home to programs needed by communities that for economic reasons produced disproportionate numbers of soldiers. In describing his initial proposal to the House, the congressman said, "Let me add that since 1981 we have suffered the Reagan-Bush and now the Bush war against the poor, and to add insult to injury, we now are asking the poor to fight while here, as a result of this fight, even the meager programs that the Congress had seen fit to preserve as a national policy will suffer because the money for those programs will be diverted to the cause of this unnecessary war."

Though González was by 1991 the chair of the powerful House Banking, Finance, and Urban Affairs Committee, and a senior member of the chamber, and though many of the concerns he expressed were recognized by Democratic and Republican members of the Congress, he was not afforded a committee hearing on his impeachment proposal. It was dismissed as a "quixotic crusade" by a man who read the Constitution too closely.

González made no apologies. "I appeal to the future for my vindication," he said. And, unfortunately, the congressman has earned a good measure of his vindication.

"Unfortunately" may seem an odd choice of words, for usually those who seek vindication welcome its arrival. But González understood that he would be proven right in the eyes of other members of Congress, the media and the citizenry only when the United States had entered the sad state of affairs that would provide clear confirmation of Thomas Jefferson's warning that "every government degenerates when trusted to the rulers of the people alone." Then, and only then, would Americans fully understand why Henry B. González had been so zealous in his defense of the Constitution. Because, of course, González was not interested in the impeachment of individual presidents; he was interested in preventing the executive branch from becoming the refuge of the "elected despots" that Jefferson and his compatriots so feared. And he was willing, as the founders intended, to use the axe of impeachment to chop the presidency down to size.

Less than one year after González died in 2000, at the age of eighty-four, a president who had come to office in the dubious circumstance of a contested election would, by exploiting the trauma and the tragedy of September 11, 2001, begin to seize unprecedented powers to spy upon American citizens, to restrict basic liberties at home and to wage undeclared wars abroad. The new president, the first in four decades to serve without the wary eyes of Henry B. González upon him, led the country into two undeclared wars and the tumultuous long-term occupations of distant lands that would cost America the lives of thousands of her precious sons and daughters and hundreds of billions of taxpayer dollars. In the guise of an undefined "war on terror," he would commit the United States to the sort of continual warfare in which James Madison warned "no nation could preserve its freedom."

The unintended consequence of George W. Bush's presidency has been to make impeachment no longer the "quixotic crusade" that was so easily dismissed when González raised the alarm in 1983, 1987 and 1991. Polls conducted early in 2006 suggested that a majority of Americans would favor impeaching the president if it was proven that he had lied about the reasons for going to war in Iraq. By the spring of the sixth year of the Bush presidency, dozens of members of Congress had signed on to a proposal to explore issues related to impeachment.

More important than the specifics of any articles of impeachment was a dawning sense on the part of liberals and conservatives that this presidency had grown too powerful, and that impeachment might indeed be the appropriate means for reining it in.

But America will not begin itself or the world anew—to paraphrase Tom Paine—until it understands that the work of impeaching George Bush or Dick Cheney or any abusive executive who might come after them ought never to be solely about the high crimes and misdemeanors of individual men. It ought to be, as Henry B. González understood—better perhaps, than any legislator of his age—the tool of constitutional renewal and the rejuvenation of the American experiment. The founders did not fear impeachment in the way that so many members of Congress did when González raised the issue. Rather, they feared what America might become if its Congress did not constrain the executive branch—and in so doing "chain the dogs of war."

This book is written in the spirit of that son of Mexican-American immigrants who served for four decades in the Congress, and in hopes of spreading his vision of impeachment as a safe and sound medicine that ought to be consumed frequently and without fear by a nation that seeks to retain the proper balance of powers and the promise of her founding. This book seeks to dispel the myths that have made so many Americans fear impeachment for reasons of politics and the orderliness of governance, so that all of us—be we citizens or mere members of Congress—will be willing to employ this gift of the founders when the need arises.

The point here is not to argue for the removal of one man, nor even of one group of men, although the nature of the moment requires a good deal of discussion about the high crimes and misdemeanors of the petty royalists who have so damaged the system of checks and balances in recent years. Rather, the point is to suggest that Jefferson was right when he wrote, "In questions of power, then, let no more be said of confidence in man, but bind him down from mischief by the chains of the Constitution," and to argue that the United States will only ever be a nation of laws—and not men—when we become as comfortable with impeaching the transient occupants of the Oval Office as was Henry B. González.

Viva Henry B.! La lucha continúa!

George Mason

"No point is of more importance than that the right of impeachment should be continued. Shall any man be above Justice?"

The Genius of Impeachment

Barbara Jordan

"If the impeachment provision in the Constitution of the United States will not reach the offenses charged here, then perhaps that eighteenth-century Constitution should be abandoned to a twentieth-century paper shredder."

CHAPTER 1

THE GENIUS OF IMPEACHMENT

No point is of more importance than that the right of impeachment should be continued. Shall any man be above Justice?

George Mason, the father of the
Bill of Rights, addressing the
Constitutional Convention of 1787

Toward the end of Woody Allen's *Annie Hall*, a film written and produced against the backdrop of that remarkable period in the mid-1970s when the process of impeachment got far enough along to force the resignation of a sitting president who did not want to face the constitutionally mandated consequences of his actions, Allen's character (Alvy Singer) is breaking up with his girlfriend (Annie). They are sorting through shared belongings when Annie spies a box of political buttons. "I guess these are all yours," she says to Alvy. "Impeach, uh, Eisenhower . . . Impeach Nixon . . . Impeach Lyndon Johnson . . . Impeach Ronald Reagan."

It was possible in 1977 to joke about impeachment because the country that had just finished the work of removing Richard Nixon and his minions from high office well understood the ancient tool and recognized it not as a political poison to be feared but rather as a healthy tonic, a cure for what ailed the American experiment. Even the major media of the country had gotten up off bended knee and acknowledged that presidents were not kings for four years, but rather servants of the people who could be held to account. Nixon's argument that the executive enjoyed extraordinary authority—"If the president orders it, that makes it legal"—had been defeated in the court of public opinion by the advice and counsel of the founders. Once again, the wisdom of James Madison prevailed, and with it the view that impeachment was an "indispensable" provision for defending the American endeavor—and the American people—"against the incapacity, negligence or perfidy of the chief Magistrate." The promise of another election, at which a wrongdoing executive might be removed, was not enough to provide such protection, as Madison had warned in his address to the Constitutional Convention that made provision for impeachment. "The limitation of the period of his service, was not a sufficient security," explained the man who would, himself, serve two full terms as the new nation's fourth president. "He might lose his capacity after his appointment. He might pervert his administration into a scheme of peculation or oppression. He might betray his trust to foreign powers . . . In the case of the Executive Magistracy which was to be administered by a single man, loss of capacity or corruption was more within the compass of probable events, and either of them might be fatal to the Republic." Gouverneur Morris, the "gentleman revolutionary" whose pen Madison credited with providing "the finish given to the style and arrangement of the Constitution," was even blunter than his compatriot. Speaking of "the necessity of impeachments," Morris asserted that only the broad power to remove executive officers—not merely for corruption and incapacity but for the far more fluidly defined act of "treachery"—would provide the essential insurance across time: "This Magistrate is not the King . . . The people are the King."

As the United States prepared to celebrate the two-hundredth anniversary of its revolt against Britain's King George III and the evils of an inherited monarchy that could not be tamed by any act save revolution, the comfort level with the bluntest tool that the founders had provided for reigning in executive excess was high. The word "impeachment" was neither foreign nor arcane. On any newsstand in the summer of 1974, a full palette of national magazines featured covers with headlines such as "The Push to Impeach," "The Fateful Vote on Impeachment," and "TV Looks at Impeachment." *Playboy* magazine asked gonzo journalist Hunter Thompson: "Are you saying you'd rather have been in the capital, covering the Senate Watergate hearings or the House Judiciary Committee debate on Nixon's impeachment, than stoned on the beach in Mexico with a bunch of freaks?" The famously drug-inclined writer responded that, yes, he had turned down a chance to party in Zihuatanejo "on the finest flower tops to be had in all of Mexico" because he just had to get to Washington. Impeachment had entered into the popular culture, earning mention everywhere from *Annie Hall* to Garry Trudeau's *Doonesbury* cartoons and the cover of *Mad* magazine to comedy bits that joked about the introduction of a new ice cream flavor: "Impeach-mint." When college students associated with the People's Bicentennial Commission reenacted the Boston Tea Party by unfurling banners calling for the impeachment of "King Richard," they declared that "The Spirit of '76 Lives!" The idea that the founders had provided for the country a tool with which to battle the imperial impulses of presidents, and that it was not merely necessary but appropriate to use it, was perhaps best summed up by Texas representative Barbara Jordan, who was one of the many previously obscure members of Congress who became what *Time* magazine referred to as the "stars" of the Watergate moment. A child of the segregated South who became the first African-American woman to represent the region in Congress, Jordan's bold and brilliant pronouncements during the House Judiciary Committee hearings on impeachment would lead to her selection in 1976, barely a decade after the passage of the Voting Rights Act, as the first African-American to deliver the keynote address at the national convention of a major American political party. It was Jordan who had released the nation's founding document from the shackles of history and make it a tool of the moment. "My faith in the Constitution is whole, it is complete, it is total. I am not going to sit here and be an idle spectator to the diminution, the subversion, the destruction of the Constitution," argued Jordan in her June 25, 1974 opening statement to the committee that declared: "If the impeachment provision in the Constitution of the United States will not reach the offenses charged here, then perhaps that eighteenth-century Constitution should be abandoned to a twentieth-century paper shredder."

Those may have been shocking words to some of her colleagues on a committee that was still not certain of its course. But they captured a sense that was rising in the land. It would come to be understood in that halcyon moment that, while Alvy Singer's impeach-'em-all politics might have been a bit over the top, the record of presidential misdeeds did not begin or end with the Nixonian lexicon of crimes and cruelties that came to be known by the name of the building where Nixon's henchmen broke into the offices of the Democratic National Committee. And there was a healthy recognition that the American experiment would be best maintained in the post-Watergate era if a higher level of scrutiny, and a higher standard of accountability, was applied to those who would occupy the Oval Office and its environs. It is no coincidence that what magazines dubbed "The Impeachment Congress"—a House and Senate that was supposedly fully absorbed by the challenge of holding a particular president to account—would in fact undertake the task of restoring the system of checks and balances that had been severely undermined by the development of what historian Arthur Schlesinger Jr. referred to as "The Imperial Presidency." Nixon's resignation may have prevented the Impeachment Congress from seeing the process of removal through to its logical conclusion, but it did not prevent that Congress from responding to the fund-raising and spending abuses of the 1972 presidential campaign by passing sweeping campaign finance reform legislation; from responding to the nightmare that was Vietnam by passing, and then overriding Nixon's veto of, a War Powers Act designed to constrain presidential warmaking; and from responding to the broader foreign policy abuses of Nixon and his recent predecessors by setting up committees to examine abuses of emergency powers by the executive branch, and to investigate collusion between the White House, intelligence agencies and U.S. corporations to assassinate foreign leaders and subvert foreign governments. No wonder, when he announced his support for impeachment, the young congressman from Harlem, Charles Rangel, mused: "Some say this is a sad day in America's history. I think it could perhaps be one of our brightest days. It could be really a test of the strength of our Constitution, because what I think it means to most Americans is that when this or any other President violates his sacred oath of office, the people are not left helpless."

The bright day would not last, however.

As the fireworks from the Bicentennial celebration faded, so too did the rebirth of the revolutionary spirit that led one of its greatest beneficiaries, a southern governor who had won his party's presidential nomination, to declare as he accepted that nomination that "it is time for our government leaders to respect the law no less than the humblest citizen, so that we can end once and for all a double standard of justice." Jimmy Carter's soft grip on the reins of power would give way to Ronald Reagan's harder pull. And the march of the imperial presidency began anew, as more and more power was concentrated in an executive branch that would, before the end of Reagan's tenure, conspire with sworn enemies of the United States to willfully violate an act of Congress that barred aid to Contra terrorists seeking to over-throw the government of Nicaragua. The congressional report on what came to be known as the Iran-Contra Affair would de-clare that Reagan bore "ultimate responsibility" for wrongdoing by aides to an administration that had exhibited "secrecy, decep-tion and disdain for the law." Yet the failure of that Congress to initiate an impeachment inquiry based on the facts of presidential wrongdoing squandered an opportunity to restore the system of checks and balances that was again under assault. In time, the po-sition of a dissenter from the congressional criticism of Reagan and his minions, then-representative Dick Cheney, would come to prevail. Other key members of the House and Senate, both Republicans and Democrats, found common ground when it came to expressing concern about abuses of power by the execu-tive branch. But Cheney, who served as vice chairman of the committee that investigated Iran-Contra, defined clear evidence of lawbreaking on the part of the executive branch as missteps—

"mistakes in judgment and nothing more," to use the Wyoming Republican's exact words—while he chastised the Congress for "abusing its power" by seeking to limit the ability of the president and his aides to spend money as they chose in support of the Contras. Cheney's dissenting statement grumbled that "Congress must recognize that effective foreign policy requires, and the Constitution mandates, the President to be the country's foreign policy leader."

Despite the fact that Cheney was wrong—the Constitution clearly and unequivocally gives the power of the purse to Congress—he would eventually find himself in a position to tip the balance of power dramatically in the direction of the executive branch. Between the time when Representative Cheney asserted that Congress should have little or no role in foreign policy and when Vice President Cheney began governing as if this were the case, the country would see the steady expansion of executive powers. As West Virginia Senator Robert Byrd observed while clutching a copy of the Constitution in 2003, it had been the purpose of successive administrations to undermine the system of checks and balances and "demolish this document which has served for more than 200 years as the foundation of this Republic." Byrd's point is well taken, especially as it recognizes that, by challenging the historic notion that the power of the purse would necessarily give Congress a defining role in setting policy, presidents and their allies were assaulting the very framework of constitutional governance. "For decades," Byrd explained, "Presidential Administrations have sought to wrap their fingers around the purse strings, push away the Congress, and ignore the Constitution. It does not matter which Administration. It does not matter the political party of the President. What matters is nothing more than raw power. Congress has it. The Executive Branch wants it—and will use any excuse to get it."

Byrd's blunt assessment of the struggle for ultimate authority was on point, especially the part about the party of the president being irrelevant when it came to power grabs. The administrations of Ronald Reagan and George Herbert Walker Bush were aggressively dismissive of constitutional mandates regarding cooperation with Congress. But so, too, was the Democratic administration of Bill Clinton. Unfortunately, constitutional purists such as Byrd have become anomalies in Washington. The post-Watergate era has been characterized by the replacement of bipartisan idealism with a partisan realpolitik that has seen most members of Congress cease to view themselves as defenders of the powers and prerogatives of the legislative branch. Rather, they have become, as Cheney was during the Reagan presidency, mere extensions of the executive branch—doing the bidding of the president when the White House is in the hands of their party, attacking the president when the White House slips from their partisan grasp.

Thus, when the noble tool of impeachment was pulled from the shelf once more—not for the purpose of challenging the high crimes and misdemeanors of Reagan but instead to highlight the low-life misbehaviors of Bill Clinton—it was not employed to constrain the executive branch but rather to achieve by legislative means what could not be accomplished at the ballot box. An honest assessment of the Clinton presidency, of the sort that has eluded the hyperpartisans of both parties, might well have found legitimate grounds for impeachment of the forty-second president in Clinton's failure to obtain congressional approval for his decision to deploy U.S. bombers and a battalion from the U.S. Army's Eighty-second Airborne Division in the Kosovo War, or perhaps in the apparent pay-to-play politics of the "Chinagate" controversy that saw money from the Chinese government flowing into political accounts associated with a president who eased restrictions on relationships between U.S. defense contractors and the Chinese military and used all the powers of his office to advocate for granting China permanent most-favored-nation trading status. But the Republican partisans who controlled the Congress in 1998 were disinclined to hold Clinton accountable for acts that benefited the same U.S. corporations that funded their campaigns, so they fought an impeachment battle so ridiculous in its focus and intents that it diminished respect for the system of checks and balances, which desperately needed revitalization. If anything, the executive branch emerged from the Clinton impeachment fight more empowered and more likely to extend that empowerment in directions that would have been unimaginable to Republicans or Democrats of the Watergate era.

George Bush may have campaigned for the presidency as a "compassionate conservative" who expressed concern about the abuses and excesses of the Clinton years and declared that the next president "must be humble" in exercising his vast powers in the international affairs arena. But the most dramatically inexperienced president in American history chose as his prince regent, his mentor and the definer of his relations with Congress an experienced hand whose views with regard to executive power were extreme even by the radical standards of the post-Watergate era. Dick Cheney never abandoned his faith, first and most fully expressed in his dissent from the Iran-Contra report, that the executive branch ought not to be hindered by the restraints put in place by the founders. Indeed, as the debate about presidential powers arose once more in the aftermath of late 2005 revelations about the Bush administration's approval of warrantless wiretaps on Americans, Cheney reminded a friendly interviewer from the *Wall Street Journal* editorial page that "if you go back and look at the minority views that were filed with the Iran-Contra report, you'll see a strong statement about the president's prerogatives and responsibilities in the foreign policy/national security area in particular."

The strong statement to which Cheney referred was his own.

History, the former Nixon aide argued, had made the executive-uber-alles position even more appropriate to 2006 than it had been to 1987 or 1973. "In the aftermath of Vietnam and Watergate . . . there was a concerted effort to place limits and restrictions on presidential authority—everything from the War Powers Act to the Hughes-Ryan Act on intelligence to stripping the president of his ability to impound funds—a series of decisions that were aimed at the time at trying to avoid a repeat of things like Vietnam or . . . Watergate," Cheney complained. "I thought they were misguided then, and have believed that given the world that we live in, that the president needs to have unimpaired executive authority."

"Unimpaired executive authority"? Now, there is a concept that fully echoes, without the least hint of irony or apology, the Nixonian view that the whims of the president should define what is legal and what is not. The U.S. Senate's watchdog on constitutional questions, Wisconsin Democrat Russ Feingold, noted the eerie parallels early in 2006, as Bush, Cheney and Attorney General Alberto Gonzales argued that the administration's policy of authorizing spying on Americans was justified—despite obvious conflicts with legal statutes and the Constitution itself—by the mere desire of the president and his acolytes to act as they might choose in a time of war. "It reminds me of what Richard Nixon said after he had left office:'Well, when the president does it that means that it is not illegal,' " explained Feingold, a ranking member of the Constitution Subcommittee of the Senate Judiciary Committee."But that is not how our constitutional democracy works."

It might seem that the United States has come full circle from the heady days of Watergate. Intriguingly, that is what defenders of the Bush administration's excesses would have us believe.They seek to foster the impression that events have necessitated the abandonment of "romantic" attachments to the faith of the founders in an American republic where the authority to set and implement policy is divided between separate and competing branches of government. "The pendulum from time to time throughout history has swung from side to side," is how Cheney puts it."Congress was pre-eminent, or the executive was pre-eminent—and as I say, I believe in this day and age, it's important that we have a strong presidency."

But, of course, the United States now has more than a strong presidency in any traditional sense.

No less an authority than John Dean, the White House counsel who turned on Nixon to speak in 1973 of "a cancer on the presidency," argues that "Bush and Cheney's presidency . . . has pushed the exclusivity of the president in matters of national security further than any predecessor, including the Nixon Administration, did."

"I'm anything but skittish about government, but I must say

this administration is truly scary and, given the times we live in, frighteningly dangerous," argues Dean, who as a fellow alumnus of the Nixon team offers an appropriately provocative challenge to Cheney's line about how "in this day and age, it's important that we have a strong presidency."

To Dean's view, Bush and Cheney "have created the most secretive presidency of my lifetime . . . far worse than during Watergate." The "worse than Watergate" line may have been dismissed by some as hyperbolic when Dean began to peddle it during the Bush administration's first term. But this former chief minority counsel to the House Judiciary Committee and associate deputy attorney general, who is today one of the nation's most respected legal commentators, is not prone to exaggeration. Dean began well before the presidential election of 2004 to construct a case against Bush and Cheney that leans heavily on concerns about the essentially unchecked power of an executive branch that operates in secret because its key players seek to conceal an agenda that serves the interests of major corporations and a neoconservative foreign policy in the pursuit of policies that are at odds not just with the practical economic and security interests of the nation and its people but with essential constitutional mandates, civil liberties protections and the system of checks and balances designed to assure that a president named George does not rule as did a King George.

Dean was ahead of the curve in sounding the alarm, perhaps because he knew the signs of executive excess better than most. But by the midpoint in the administration's second term, his was no longer a lonely voice in the wilderness of what he accurately referred to as "the Bush and Cheney presidency." Popular journals of opinion such as *Harper's* and *The Nation* featured calls for impeachment, with the latter highlighting the arguments of another veteran of the Watergate wars, former New York representative Elizabeth Holtzman, who wrote early in 2006: "Finally, it has started. People have begun to speak of impeaching President George W. Bush—not in hushed whispers but openly, in newspapers, on the Internet, in ordinary conversations and even in Congress. As a former member of Congress who sat on the House Judiciary Committee during the impeachment proceedings against President Richard Nixon, I believe they are right to do so."

Recalling "the sinking feeling in the pit of my stomach" that she had felt when it became clear that Nixon would need to be impeached, Holtzman wrote, "At the time, I hoped that our committee's work would send a strong signal to future Presidents that they had to obey the rule of law. I was wrong."

With the deliberate approach that earned her international attention and respect during the Watergate hearings, Holtzman identified the turning point at which disagreement and discomfort with the Bush-Cheney administration metastasized into advocacy for its removal:

Like many others, I have been deeply troubled by Bush's breathtaking scorn for our international treaty obligations under the United Nations Charter and the Geneva Conventions. I have also been disturbed by the torture scandals and the violations of US criminal laws at the highest levels of our government they may entail. These concerns have been compounded by growing evidence that the President deliberately misled the country into the war in Iraq. But it wasn't until the most recent revelations that President Bush directed the wiretapping of hundreds, possibly thousands, of Americans, in violation of the Foreign Intelligence Surveillance Act (FISA)—and argued that, as Commander in Chief, he had the right in the interests of national security to override our country's laws—that I felt the same sinking feeling in my stomach as I did during Watergate.

As a matter of constitutional law, these and other misdeeds constitute grounds for the impeachment of President Bush. A President, any President, who maintains that he is above the law—and repeatedly violates the law—thereby commits high crimes and misdemeanors, the constitutional standard for impeachment and removal from office. A high crime or misdemeanor is an archaic term that means a serious abuse of power, whether or not it is also a crime, that endangers our constitutional system of government.

While Holtzman's stance, like that of Dean, could be respected from an intellectual standpoint, it could also be dismissed by defenders of the president as an exercise in nostalgia—old warriors reliving the experience of ancient battles by comparing and constrasting them with contemporary struggles.

But the return of the word "impeachment" to the national discourse in late 2005 and early 2006 was not just a case of those who had fought to hold Nixon to account returning to the barricades in defense of the Constitution. Members of Congress who were barely old enough to vote in the mid-1970s were joining the fight, as well—and they were doing so not just in the spirit of 1974 but in the spirit of 1776. The maverick Feingold, who was the only Democrat in the Senate to vote with Republicans to hear all the evidence for Clinton's impeachment, now observed that Bush was acting more like a sovereign monarch than an elected leader. "We have a system of law," Feingold said when the administration refused to stop ordering federal agencies to conduct warrantless wiretaps on Americans. "He just can't make up the law . . . It would turn George Bush not into President George Bush, but King George Bush."

That reference to King George, always more appropriate to a discussion of impeachment than comparisons with Nixon, Reagan, Clinton or similarly malignant occupiers of the Oval Office, gave the discussion a perspective, and an energy, that was needed. Debates about impeachment ought never to be merely technical. They can never begin and end with recitations of the relevant statutes, the particulars of the high crimes or the minutiae of the misdemeanors. In a country founded on the cusp of the enlightenment—with the pamphleteer Tom Paine crying: "O Ye that love mankind! Ye that dares oppose not only the tyranny but the tyrant, stand forth!"—there must always be more to talk of removing the miscreant than the explication of his unsuitability. There must be principle as well as pragmatism. And so Feingold got it right when he responded to a 2006 State of the Union address that was riddled with executive excuse-making about wiretaps and spy schemes: "As the President said, we must always be clear in our principles. So let us be clear: We cherish the great and noble principle of freedom, we will fight to keep it, and we will hold this President—and anyone who violates those freedoms—accountable for their actions. In a nation built on freedom, the President is not a king, and no one is above the law."

Thus, we find ourselves at that rare and remarkable point

where the proper parameters of a national discussion regarding impeachment have been put in place.

The bill of particulars against George W. Bush and Dick Cheney is a long and detailed one—from the misuse and misstatement of intelligence to imagine a case for war with Iraq, to the approval of the abuse of prisoners and torture, to the leaking of information intended to harm the reputations of the administration's critics, to warrantless wiretapping, to the deliberate refusals by members of the administration to cooperate with Congress. This text will examine the charges against the president and vice president, as any book on impeachment written in times such as these must. But this book is about more than the high crimes and misdemeanors of one president.

This is a book about the genius of impeachment—and about the need to reclaim and reuse, without the pretense of apology, the most vital tool handed to us by the founders for the defense of our basic liberties and of the Constitution that guarantees the continuity of this American experiment. That Constitution contains no less than six specific references to impeachment. They were placed there for a reason. There is no question of the intention of those who freed what were once colonies from the despotism of a distant and disengaged monarch. They did not want the guardians of their hard-won independence to know, let alone to tolerate, any form of tyranny. "An elective despotism was not the government we fought for," recalled Thomas Jefferson, who warned always that "the powers of government should be so divided and balanced among general bodies of magistracy, as that no one could transcend their legal limits without being effectually checked and restrained by the others."

If the official checks and balances fail, Jefferson believed, then a citizenry, as enlightened as it is enraged, must set the country right. "I know of no safe depository of the ultimate powers of the society but the people themselves," explained Jefferson, "and if we think them not enlightened enough to exercise their control with a wholesome discretion, the remedy is not to take it from them but to inform their discretion by education. This is the true corrective of abuses of constitutional power."

It is time to renew the familiarity of the American people not merely with the concept of impeachment, but with its glorious potential to serve as the truest corrective of abuses of constitutional power, and the surest weapon in the defense of the republic.

Edmund Burke as depicted by James Gillray in 1791

*"It is a contradiction in terms, it is blasphemy in religion, it is wickedness
in politics, to say that any man can have arbitrary power."*

CHAPTER 2

A LIVE INSTRUMENT
OF THE CONSTITUTION

It is by this process, that magistracy which tries and controls all other things, is itself tried and controlled. Other constitutions are satisfied with making good subjects; this is a security for good governors. It is by this tribunal, that statesmen, who abuse their power, are accused by statesmen, and tried by statesmen, not upon the niceties of a narrow jurisprudence, but upon the enlarged and solid principles of state morality. It is here, that those, who by the abuse of power have violated the spirit of law, can never hope for protection from any of its forms:—it is here, that those, who have refused to conform themselves to its perfections, can never hope to escape through any of its defects. It ought, therefore, my lords, to become our common care to guard this your precious deposit, rare in its use, but powerful in its effect, with a religious vigilance, and never to suffer it to be either discredited or antiquated.

Edmund Burke, opening the
impeachment trial of Warren
Hastings before the House of Lords,
1787

The first formal effort to impeach a government official for manipulating intelligence and deceiving elected legislators and the
people of his country on behalf of the neoconservative project to
invade and occupy Iraq did not come in the United States. Fit-
tingly, it was an endeavor of a Welsh parliamentarian serving in
the British House of Commons who, rather as a knight of
Arthurian legend drawing forth "the brand Excalibur," pulled the
parliamentary power to impeach from the encasements of history
and official neglect to confront the cruelties of a ruler no longer
constrained by the rule of law.

On May 1, 2005, the conservative *Times* of London revealed
what came to be known as "the Downing Street Memo," official
notes from meetings of British Prime Minister Tony Blair and his
aides that detailed the machinations leading up to an illegal and
immoral war. The article on the leaked documents, by the award-
winning journalist Michael Smith, began: "A secret document
from the heart of government reveals today that Tony Blair pri-
vately committed Britain to war with Iraq and then set out to
lure Saddam Hussein into providing the legal justification." The
notes confirmed that Blair had, in conversations with President
Bush, committed British support for "regime change" by force in
Iraq, despite warnings from Lord Goldsmith, Britain's attorney
general, that such action could be illegal. They also revealed that,
in response to concerns expressed by British foreign secretary
Jack Straw that the case for war was "thin" as "Saddam was not
threatening his neighbours and his WMD capability was less than
that of Libya, North Korea or Iran," a plan was developed to "create" conditions to justify a war.

The method for the creation of those conditions, according
to the text of the memo published that day in the *Times,* was

blunt. The official notations explained that "the intelligence and facts were being fixed around the policy." In other words, as Sir Menzies Campbell, who at the time served as the foreign affairs spokesman for Britain's Liberal Democratic Party, said upon being apprised of the contents of the leaked memo, "[Blair's government had] agreed to an illegal regime change with the Bush administration. It set out to create the justification for going to war. It was to be war by any means."

The details revealed by the Downing Street Memo, along with further reporting by Smith and other journalists who pursued the story with a combination of skepticism and zeal rarely exhibited by American reporters in recent years, shocked Britain, and undoubtedly contributed to the decline of Blair's political fortunes in national voting four days after the *Times* headlined the story. But, while most members of the House of Commons batted the revelations around like a political football, one parliamentarian recognized that this news validated a year-long struggle he had waged to hold Blair to account.

Adam Price, the member of parliament for the Welsh constituency of Carmarthen East and Dinefwr who had been honored by Britain's *Spectator* magazine as the "Parliamentary Inquisitor of the Year," had begun arguing in 2004 that evidence of Blair's employment of a "dodgy dossier" to make the "case" for war merited the ultimate sanction. A war had been launched, the government of a foreign land had been violently deposed, British soldiers had died in combat. If all of this had been based on lies, or whatever other name might attach in polite company to the manipulation of facts and the deception of the people's representatives, as Price believed to be the case, and as the Downing Street notes would confirm, then Blair must be held to account—fully and formally—for what the parliamentarian described as "an organised deception to win over a sceptical parliament and public to the military action he had long ago promised his ally Mr. Bush."

Price had met in the summer of 2004 with members of parliament from his own party, the Welsh nationalist Plaid Cymru, as well as members of the Scottish Nationalist Party, both of which had opposed the war, and secured their support for an impeachment bid. This was no casual matter for Price. He intended to dot every "i" and cross every "t." To do this, the parliamentarian knew he would need help. It was at this point that Dan Plesch's mobile phone rang. An academic and author whose incisive analyses of the arguments made by Bush and Blair for going to war had earned him a national reputation as one of the prime minister's sharpest critics, Plesch had months earlier written an article for Britain's *Guardian* newspaper—headlined: "There is always impeachment"—in which he argued that "there are some MPs who believe that a great crime has been committed over Iraq—a crime without precedent in modern British history. If their concern is as serious as they say, then impeachment is a tool they should use. At the very least, raising impeachment on the floor of the Commons would be an act that would reverberate around the world." Price told the research fellow at Birkbeck College of his desire to launch an impeachment bid, and of his need for a scholarly ally. The game was afoot. "Over the summer, Adam and I researched impeachment," Plesch recalled. "There were times when we felt like kids in a real-life Harry Potter adventure, turning the pages of 300-year-old books to discover a lost treasure of great power that we can use to preserve our freedom."

Price picked well when he contacted Plesch. The academic's appropriate delight in the reclaiming of that "lost treasure" reflects the attitude that is essential to any useful embrace of impeachment. To see the procedure as dangerous or even precious, as a weapon to be employed only in the most dire and defensive of circumstances, is to blunt the edges of the sword. If impeachment is a tool that holds leaders to account, then it has to be what Plesch described in the arguments he would eventually employ to promote the cause of Blair's removal: "a live instrument of the constitution." To fit that description, impeachment must be both at the ready and readily employed—not for the simple settling of scores, not for political gain, but for the defense of freedoms that are ever in the balance.

That was the intent of those who forged the sword of impeachment in a time when the Arthurian legends did not seem particularly ancient.

Impeachment is not an American innovation. This "last resort for holding ministers to account" was, as Plesch well recalls, "invented in England before the wars of the roses, then reinforced by the Scottish parliamentary law of trying the king's ministers for giving false advice. Impeachment is a great British export—famously to the United States, but also as far afield as the Philippines and Iran."

To understand the history of impeachment is to recognize the development of the rule of law as it is applied in a parliamentary democracy. So it should come as little surprise that the roots of impeachment as it is today known can be traced directly to the fourteenth century, when the British House of Commons, or Parliament, began to flex its muscles as a force with the authority to apply the rule of law even to associates of the king. The tool that commoners used to remove corrupt and cruel members of the aristocracy, along with their untitled partners in crime, was impeachment. What is, perhaps, surprising is how little the process has changed from the days when fourteenth-century parliamentarians gingerly challenged the nobility. The impeachment procedures that are enshrined in the American Constitution are, as Alexander Hamilton noted in the Federalist Papers, "borrowed" from those used as long ago as 1376, when the first speaker of the House of Commons, Peter de la Mare, a former toll collector who had served as the sheriff of Herefordshire, took the unprecedented step of initiating proceedings against Lord William Latimer—a particularly crooked peer of the realm who was then serving as chamberlain to an ailing and politically weakened King Edward III—along with Latimer's partner in various shady transactions, Richard Lyons, who was the king's financial agent.

While the roots of the word "impeachment" can be followed back to a Late Latin term meaning "to fetter"—*impedicare*—it was a Middle English variation, *empechen,* that was first recorded in the fourteenth century as a reference to the act of bringing charges against a powerful wrongdoer. That is precisely what the so-called Good Parliament of 1376, serving as the very rough antecedent to what would become the contemporary U.S. House of Representatives, did when it followed Peter de la Mare's lead and determined that Latimer and Lyons should be punished for raiding the public treasury—they stole the wool staple from Calais—in the service of their personal enrichment.

The language, tentative in character and deferent as it may have been to royal prerogatives, was not so very different in spirit or intent from an article of impeachment that might today be endorsed by the U.S. House. Citing the nobleman's wrongdoing, the Good Parliament made its demand: "Wherefore we pray and require you on behalf of the king and the council of parliament that the said lord Latimer be arrested and kept safely for all the said trespasses and forfeits, until he has made satisfaction to the king for his misdeeds; and that the said Richard Lyons be judged as he deserves upon the points and articles put against him, which he cannot reasonably deny."

There was no great doubt about where the Good Parliament's demand was directed. In the fourteenth century, a nobleman was not likely to submit to summary judgment on charges brought by commoners, let alone allow himself to be tried by mere elected officials, as Lord Latimer was quick to suggest. While the House of Commons was asserting that it had the authority to impeach a nobleman, just as the lower and more representative chamber of the U.S. Congress today enjoys the authority to impeach members of the executive and judiciary branches of the government, a trial on those charges would be held only in the House of Lords, in much the same manner that impeachment trials would come to be conducted in the U.S. Senate. As Matthew Romney observed more than six centuries later in a reflection on impeachment published in the University of Utah's *Hinckley Journal of Politics,*

Lord Latimer asked that written charges be submitted and that he be granted counsel and time to prepare a defense. As a member of the House of Lords, Latimer was asking for a trial before the Lords to determine his guilt or innocence, just as would be required for a common-law offense. Though he was not ultimately granted the first request for written charges, he was granted his second and third requests and was allowed to defend himself before the Lords, thus introducing the element of intra-parliamentary rivalry into the impeachment process. More importantly, however, the Lords' concern for the legitimacy of charges, procedures and evidence, as well as other legal processes, would become a check on the highly politicized environment of the Commons . . . By adding a trial in a separate body to impeachment by the Commons, a first in English history, the Parliament of 1376 gave the impeachment process a legal framework which would become one of the roots of its legitimacy for centuries to come.

Latimer and Lyons were briefly imprisoned. Additionally, Alice Perrers, the royal mistress whose hand was clearly evident in the corruptions of the impeached pair, was—despite a plea from the king, whose reputation had been badly diminished by costly and generally unsuccessful military misadventures abroad and the mismanagement of a domestic public health crisis, a new outbreak of the bubonic plague in 1374 and 1375—banished from the royal court. The first moment of impeachment-inspired reform would be brief. The death of the Black Prince—a rebellious son of King Edward who, in his capacity as the Prince of Wales, had lent legitimacy to the Good Parliament—shortly after the impeachment proceedings shifted power away from the Commons. The Good Parliament of 1376 was dissolved, to be replaced by the Bad Parliament of 1377. Fortunes were quickly reversed. Latimer and Lyons were released from prison and recalled to the court, while Peter de la Mare was himself imprisoned in Nottingham Castle by the nefarious John of Gaunt. Before the year was done, Edward III was dead, and de la Mare was released from

prison, pardoned by Richard II, returned to parliament and restored to his position as speaker.

Those who fear the political repercussions of the impeachment process would do well to make note of the risks taken by
Peter de la Mare to establish the precedent that the people's representatives have the authority to hold to account "evil councillors-
lors" and, by extension, the most powerful figures in the realm.
The immediate successors to de la Mare, though they were well
aware of the dangers of doing so, continued to forge the sword of
accountability. In 1386, as they were going about the work of removing yet another royal chancellor, the Earl of Suffolk, the
catch-all phrase "high crimes and misdemeanors"—which in the
earl's case involved everything from "squandering away the public treasure" to "procuring offices for persons who were unfit, and
unworthy of them"—was added to the lexicon of impeachment,
where it remains to this day. Impeaching the king's chancellor did
not sit well with Richard II, however, and in 1388, the monarch
signalled that he did not believe the Commons could impeach a
royal aide without royal consent. What followed was not a John
Sirica moment. Where the federal judge who reigned in the excesses of the American presidency in 1973 did so by upholding
the authority of the legislative branch to police an executive
branch headed by Richard Nixon, the judges of Richard II's
realm sided with the sovereign at whose "good pleasure" they
served—declaring that impeachments could only advance with
royal approval. In what even this writer will acknowledge might
accurately be described as "legislative excess," the Commons
pushed back by impeaching the judges and jailing them.

This turbulent state of affairs—in which an uncertain Parliament flexed the muscle of impeachment and the monarchy ac-

cepted or repulsed the challenges depending at least to some extent on the targets of the inquisitions—continued into the fifteenth century. But as the power of Parliament waned and the Tudor dynasty reasserted royal authority, impeachment fell into disuse. Thus began a pattern, seen in Britain and the United States to this day, of impeachment flourishing and then being, in Dan Plesch's words, all but "lost to history"—only to be plucked from the dustbin in moments of national crisis. Such was the case in the 1620s, when the newly enthroned King Charles I dealt with the monarchy's incessant financial problems by repeatedly dissolving Parliaments that, employing what would come to be known as "the power of the purse," attempted to exercise control over the sovereign by limiting grants of public funds for European wars in which Charles sought to intervene on behalf of royal relatives. After summoning and dissolving three sittings of Parliament between 1625 and 1629, Charles simply stopped summoning them, and the legislative branch of government did not function for more than a decade. Mixing religion and politics into a uniquely toxic brew, Charles championed "the divine right of kings" as justification for his assumption of absolute power during what would come to be known as the Eleven Years Tyranny. Only when festering rebellions against the introduction of Anglicanism to Scotland and unwarranted taxation in Britain erupted was Charles forced to summon a new Parliament in hopes of funding the armies he would need to maintain his reign.

The House of Commons was not in a mood to rubber-stamp the madness of King Charles, however, and the legislative branch took a number of steps to end the era of absolute power, among them the restoration of impeachment as a tool for fighting abuses of power by royal agents. The first target of the reinvig-

orated power of impeachment was Thomas Wentworth, first Earl
of Strafford, the king's principal adviser, who proposed all-out
war against the Scots by urging Charles to reject the counsel of
Parliament and "go on with a vigorous war as you first designed,
loose and absolved from all rules of government," and calling
upon the king to employ his armies "to reduce this kingdom . . ."
Charles bought into the strategy, appointing the tyrannical Strafford to head the army, which the earl proposed to finance by
forcing the citizens of London to pay new taxes and raiding the
Tower of London to seize bullion that had been stored there by
private citizens. Strafford's schemes failed both militarily and politically, and he was charged by the House of Commons with the
"high misdemeanour" of attempting to subvert the fundamental
laws of the kingdom. The House of Lords absolved Strafford, but
the Commons was not giving up. By a vote of 204 to 59, it passed
a bill of attainder calling for the execution of the man who had
come to symbolize the absolute monarchy of Charles. The people sided with their parliament as Britain edged toward civil war.
The Lords relented and, after a bitter power struggle, Charles
abandoned his essential aide to execution on London's Tower
Hill before a crowd estimated at 200,000. In less than a decade,
Charles himself would be executed as the monarchy was over-
thrown and the "Lord General of the Parliamentary Army,"
Oliver Cromwell, assumed something akin to royal authority as
the "Lord Protector of England," Scotland and Ireland.

   In another decade, the monarchy would be restored, with the
son of the executed king, Charles II, installed at the head of a new
royal court that would accept and even encourage the development of modern parliamentary politics. Impeachment was very
much a part of this new politics. In an era when the lines of polit-

ical distinction between branches of government began to be drawn, impeachment came to be seen, in the words of one commentator on the affairs of state, as a primary "instrument of parliamentary resistance to the crown." In 1681, during a struggle between the House of Commons and the House of Lords over the impeachment of one Edward Fitzharris, the standard was finally and firmly established by the Parliament: "That it is the undoubted right of the Commons to impeach before the Lords any Peer or commoner for treason or any other crime or misdemeanour, and that the refusal of the Lords to proceed in Parliament upon such impeachment is a denial of justice and a violation of the constitution of Parliament."

Eight years later, in 1689, the House of Commons would officially declare impeachment to be "the chief institution for the preservation of the government."

Impeachment became, by the early years of the eighteenth century, so well established in the politics of the British Isles that Jonathan Swift would make appropriate reference to the procedure in *Gulliver's Travels,* his satirical assessment of the abasement of political power in countries not so very different from the European states of the 1720s, when he was writing. Swift's traveler, Lemuel Gulliver, is confronted by the threat of trial for high treason: "This Lord, in conjunction with Flimnap the High Treasurer, whose Enmity against you is notorious on account of his Lady, Limtoc the General, Lalcon the Chamberlain, and Balmuff the grand Justiciary, have prepared Articles of Impeachment against you, for Treason, and other capital Crimes."

Britain's last great impeachment trial played out in the House of Lords at precisely the same time that the founders of the new United States were forging a constitution that would recognize impeachment as an essential tool for balancing the powers of the three branches of government they were establishing. In Britain, where issues of empire were being debated with new energy, and with a dawning recognition that the Parliament had a duty to control the brutal behaviors of the empire's colonial functionaries, impeachment proceedings were brought in 1786 against the governor-general of India, a British East India Company retainer named Warren Hastings. Charged with employing excess force to demand subsidies from the rulers of the north Indian states of Varanasi and Oudh, and with personal and political corruption, Hastings was recalled from Calcutta to London for a spectacular trial before the House of Lords that would last seven years. The man behind the charges, and the chief manager of the impeachment trial, was Edmund Burke, the British statesman who had first attempted to impose parliamentary oversight via legislation that would have established a London-based board of independent commissioners to govern India—as opposed to the murky public-private partnership of the British government and the East India Company. When King George III balked at Burke's bill and successfully pressured the House of Lords to reject it, the parliamentarian turned to impeachment as a method for establishing the authority of the House of Commons in matters of empire. The Hastings trial was a sensation; published accounts at the time reported that "the streets were kept clear by cavalry. The peers, robed in gold and ermine, were marshalled by the heralds under garter King-at-arms. The judges, in their vestments of state, attended to give advice on points of law."

At the close of the Hastings trial in 1795, the Lords refused to convict the man Burke described as "the captain-general of iniquity." But the principle of parliamentary oversight of the colonial

endeavor, which Burke had set out to establish, had begun finally
to be accepted as a political and practical necessity. Here was a
classic example of the power of impeachments, even when unsuccessful, to address patterns of corruption and executive excess
that might otherwise go unchallenged. Here, too, was evidence of
the essential role of the impeachment process in upholding the
rule of law. As Burke declared in the early stages of the Hastings
trial, "Law and arbitrary power are in eternal enmity. Name me a
magistrate, and I will name property; name me power, and I will
name protection. It is a contradiction in terms, it is blasphemy in
religion, it is wickedness in politics, to say that any man can have
arbitrary power. In every patent of office the duty is included. For
what else does a magistrate exist? To suppose for power is an ab-
surdity in idea. Judges are guided and governed by the eternal
laws of justice, to which we are all subject. We may bite our
chains, if we will, but we shall be made to know ourselves, and be
taught that man is born to be governed by law; and he that will
substitute will in the place of it is an enemy to God."

It was against this backdrop that the delegates to the Constitutional Convention met in Philadelphia to set the outlines of the
government of the new United States. Legislatures in the former
British colonies arrayed along the east coast of the North American continent had impeached officials as early as 1635, when the
general assembly of Virginia took action against John Harvey, the
colony's royal governor. One of the founders of the American experiment, John Adams, had participated in an impeachment trial
in 1774, that of Massachusetts Supreme Court chief justice Peter
Oliver, who had been appointed to his position by Governor
Thomas Hutchinson, a relative of Oliver's by marriage who
made the selection in an effort to control the judiciary. Another

founder, Thomas Jefferson, had himself faced the threat of impeachment by Virginia legislators who felt that Jefferson, who served during the Revolutionary War as governor of that state, had poorly managed its defenses.

The delegates who began gathering to draft a constitution on "the second Monday in May" of 1787 had little disagreement about the role impeachment would play in the republic. Fresh from a revolt against the colonial rule of a distant and unaccountable monarch, they did not intend to allow the development of similar circumstances under their watch. It was the purpose of the founders to constrain, rather than empower, the executive branch of government and, for this reason, as Matthew Romney has noted, their framework for impeachment had "a distinct republican shape—it was limited to officeholders, for offenses outside the jurisdiction of the common law, with a punishment limited to removal and disqualification." But that did not mean that there was no debate. Edmund Randolph's Virginia Plan, with its fifteen propositions that formed the starting point for the convention's deliberations, featured a mechanism for impeachment of any officer of the federal government but imagined that trials would be conducted by the federal judiciary. Alexander Hamilton, inspired by the model of his own state's New York Court for the Trial of Impeachments and the Correction of Errors, countered with a plan that would have impeachment trials conducted by the "Chief or Judge of the Superior Court of Law of each State." Fearing conflicts of interest that might develop if jurists appointed by a president found themselves sitting in judgment on that president and his appointees, various compromises were proposed, with the Pennsylvanian Gouverneur Morris making the successful case for trial by the Senate, which would be the upper chamber of the new Congress. Morris, who had broken with his own royalist family to embrace the patriot's cause as a young man, then joined in the debate over what would constitute an impeachable offense, suggesting that "the Executive ought therefore to be impeachable for treachery; Corrupting his electors, and incapacity . . ." Another delegate, Hugh Williamson of North Carolina, proposed that the executive "be removable on impeachment and conviction of malpractice and neglect of duty." These broad definitions were reduced during the debates of that hot summer to, according to notations made in early September by James Madison, "treason and bribery."

The narrow definition did not sit well with George Mason, the author of the Virginia Declaration of Rights, who was the convention's most ardent advocate for enumerating the rights of citizens and their elected representatives to constrain the government that was being created. "Why is the provision restrained to Treason & bribery only? Treason as defined in the Constitution will not reach many great and dangerous offences. Hastings is not guilty of Treason," argued Morris, referencing the target of Burke and the British Parliament. "Attempts to subvert the Constitution may not be Treason as above defined. As bills of attainder which have saved the British Constitution are forbidden, it is the more necessary to extend the power of impeachments." In addition to treason and bribery, Mason argued, "maladministration" needed be listed as an impeachable offense. When James Madison suggested that the term was so vague as to invite abuse, Madison's own notes recall that "Col. Mason withdrew 'maladministration' & substitutes 'other high crimes & misdemeanors agst. the State.' "

With this final borrowing from the British, the rough form

of the constitutional provisions for impeachment was in place. In the document that took effect in 1789, and that is today the oldest written national constitution still in use, those provisions were spelled out in two separate amendments.

Article I, which establishes the legislative branch of the government as a congress consisting of a house of representatives and a senate, confirms in Section Two that "the House of Representatives shall choose their Speaker and other Officers; and shall have the sole Power of Impeachment," and in Section Three that "the Senate shall have the sole Power to try all Impeachments. When sitting for that Purpose, they shall be on Oath or Affirmation. When the President of the United States is tried, the Chief Justice shall preside: And no Person shall be convicted without the Concurrence of two thirds of the Members present." Establishing the parameters of punishment, Section Three also declares, "Judgment in Cases of Impeachment shall not extend further than to removal from Office, and disqualification to hold and enjoy any Office of honor, Trust or Profit under the United States: but the Party convicted shall nevertheless be liable and subject to Indictment, Trial, Judgment and Punishment, according to Law."

Article II, the much shorter statement that defines the "executive Power" of the government as being "vested in a President of the United States of America" who "shall hold his Office during the Term of four Years" and to a much lesser extent in "the Vice President, chosen for the same Term," states in Section Four that "the President, Vice President and all civil Officers of the United States, shall be removed from Office on Impeachment for, and Conviction of, Treason, Bribery, or other high Crimes and Misdemeanors."

So there it was. The new United States had defined impeachment, constitutionally, as an essential component of the American enterprise. It was here that borrowing from Britain gave way to lending to the new countries that would seek to emulate the structures established by the former colonies that had broken the grip of monarchy and embraced the rule of law. As the British academic Dan Plesch would note with reference to the eighteenth-century trial of the colonialist Warren Hastings, "Informed by this trial, the founders of the US Constitution used the English example as the basis for US impeachment law. From here it spread quite widely, and in late 2004 it is part of political life as far afield as Iran, India, Nevada and Colombia."

Through its broad influence beyond the borders of the United States, the Constitution crafted by Madison and Morris would offer the protection and promise of impeachment to peoples around the world who, in their borrowings from what would become a defining document for nation builders, have made impeachment a vital part of politics, from Brazil (where a president was impeached in 1992) to Lithuania (where a president was impeached in 2004) to Paraguay (where a president was impeached in 1999) to the Philippines (where a president was impeached in 2000) to South Korea (where a president was impeached in 2004) to Venezuela (where a president was impeached in 1993) to Vanuatu (where a president was impeached in 2004). In the spring of 2006, as Americans engaged in tentative discussions about whether to brush off what Lord Bryce referred to as "the heaviest artillery in the congressional arsenal," congresses, parliaments and legislatures in Malawi, Nigeria, Thailand and the Philippines were considering or actually acting upon articles of impeachment, and it seemed like it would be only a matter of time before the National Assembly of Iraq or Afghanistan's Wolesi Jirga took advantage of the impeachment powers afforded each of them in newly drafted constitutions.

Yet, as Great Britain's Dan Plesch explained when he first raised the issue of impeaching Tony Blair in his article of January 2004, impeachment had by the first years of the twenty-first century been all but discarded by the guardians of his own country's experiment with democracy. "Say the word 'impeachment' and people think of Bill Clinton and Monica Lewinsky or, before that, Richard Nixon," Plesch wrote. "In fact, it is an English invention. The men who wrote the United States constitution borrowed it from the House of Commons, where it was used for much of the 17th and 18th centuries. But while impeachment has remained in print in the US constitution, in England it has been lost to history."

Plesch informed readers who might have been shocked to learn that impeachment carried a "Made in Britain" label that "there are reasons why impeachment has fallen out of use in the UK: the ability of the normal courts to try those accused of major corruption; the custom that ministers found to have lied to parliament resign; and the use of a no-confidence vote to remove a government and precipitate an election. These all provide good safeguards in usual circumstances."

But "in the case of Iraq," argued Plesch, "there may well be an argument for bringing back impeachment."

The first step in so doing was taken by a member of Blair's own Labour Party, Peter Kilfoyle, a member of Parliament for Liverpool. Kilfoyle, who had served as a defense minister before quitting Blair's Cabinet and emerging as a vocal critic of the prime minister's Iraq policies, asked the House of Commons library for a briefing on whether impeachment was still an option. Though the last serious move to impeach a British official had been a failed attempt in 1848 to hold Viscount Palmerston to account for entering into a secret treaty with Russia against Turkey, Kilfoyle was informed that the "ancient procedure of impeachment" remained a legitimate "exercise of the law of parliament."

In the summer of 2004, after a pair of inquiries set up by the British government to examine the use and misuse of intelligence relating to Saddam Hussein's supposed possession of weapons of mass destruction prior to the invasion of Iraq—the Hutton Inquiry and the Butler Report—highlighted the fact that key arguments made by Blair to justify the war had been based on a so-called dodgy dossier, calls to hold the prime minister to account grew louder. Though Blair and his allies claimed that they had been vindicated by the inquiries, former foreign secretary Douglas Hurd captured the frustration with the prime minister's "What, me Worry?" response when he observed, "We should be used to it by now. The prime minister stands at the despatch box, radiating his personal brand of righteousness, using every trick of the trade to justify what cannot now be justified. He defends himself against an accusation which no one makes, that he acted in bad faith. We all know that he deceived himself first. He says that he accepts the Butler report, but at the same time holds to the decision to invade Iraq; but the report finally knocks away the main argument he gave us for that decision."

Hurd, one of the great British parliamentarians of the twentieth century, was now safely ensconced in the House of Lords. But Adam Price, the Welsh inquisitor who entered Parliament after the first election of the twenty-first century, wanted to do more than merely fume about the arrogance of the prime minister. Price wanted to act. At his urging, Plesch and another re-spected academic, Glen Rangwala—a Cambridge University scholar who had revealed in 2003 that a key dossier used by Blair and his aides to make the "case" for war had been based on "intel-ligence" plagiarized from a postgraduate student's thesis and dated magazine articles—began researching whether Blair's ac-tions merited impeachment. In August 2004 they produced "A Case to Answer," a report that relied on the prime minister's own statements and evidence disclosed in the Hutton Inquiry and the Butler Report to argue that Blair had:

- Made twenty-eight statements about Iraq's weapons that were unsupported by the intelligence assessments available to him. (The statements will be familiar to Americans who listened to the Bush administration's arguments before the war: "We know that Saddam Hussein has stockpiles of major amounts of chemical and biological weapons"; "[Hussein] is developing weapons of mass destruction and we cannot leave him to do so unchecked. He is a threat to his own people and to the region and, if allowed to develop these weapons, a threat to us also"; "[Iraq has] enough chemical and biological weapons remaining to devas-tate the entire Gulf region.")
- Failed to disclose available counterevidence, or failed to ensure that claims were verified on twelve occasions.
- Failed to withdraw material later found to be false.
- Entered into an agreement with the United States without the consent of the Cabinet, Parliament or the people of the United Kingdom.

On the basis of the evidence presented, the report concluded that the prime minister was duty-bound to explain why he:

- Failed to resign after misleading Parliament and the United Kingdom.
- Made a secret agreement with a foreign power.
- Undermined the the United Kingdom's body of constitutional laws
- Countenanced negligence and incompetence.

Assuming that Blair would not willingly respond, Plesch argued that impeachment was in order.

"It is unheard of for a minister to knowingly deceive Parliament and the public and to refuse to resign," he explained. "Blair seriously misled and deceived the public over Iraq and there can be no greater offence for a Prime Minister. Impeachment is the only way to ensure that Tony Blair doesn't get away with this."

"A Case to Answer" attracted enthusiastic praise from unexpected quarters. Writing in London's *Daily Telegraph* newspaper, the bible of the British political establishment, Boris Johnson, a Conservative Party member of Parliament and the editor of *Spectator* magazine, promoted "A Case to Answer" as essential summer reading: "Put down *The Da Vinci Code*. Jack in the Grisham. Let Jilly Cooper turn yellow and wilt by the pool. I have before me a beach read more shocking than the schlockiest bonkbuster. It is only 80 pages, so you ought to be able to knock it off after even the most vinous siesta. Like all the best holiday reads, the idea is simple. A couple of academics have taken the words of Tony Blair on the subject of Saddam Hussein and his weapons of mass destruction. They have culled each top-spun, souped-up, over-egged quotation, and set it side by side with what the Prime Minister was actually being told about those WMD. You are left at the end feeling angry and bewildered that Blair should take us all for such mugs."

To Johnson's view, there was indeed a case to answer. "At every stage, Blair upgrades hypothesis into fact," the conservative parliamentarian growled.

He said that Saddam's WMD posed a threat to the region; the intelligence said otherwise. He said the WMD programme was 'growing'; he had no such evidence available to him. He said that the UN inspectors were reporting that illicit weapons did exist, when they merely said that the materials were unaccounted for, and he failed to make the distinction clear. Why did he do it? Why at so many times and in so many places did he take such a huge gamble with reality? Because he thought he could get away with it. He thought it overwhelmingly likely that something would turn up, and that in the excitement his exaggerations would be forgotten. He has been caught out. He has allowed the method of the spin doctors to corrupt his presentation of the most vital public information; except that in this case you can't blame the spin doctors. It was Blair, Blair, Blair.

He was broadly right about Saddam; he was, in my view, broadly right about the war, though in retrospect we should have insisted on better particulars about American plans for post-war Iraq. He was utterly wrong to use such dishonest means of persuasion. He treated Parliament and the public with contempt, and that is

why he deserves to be impeached: that is, to be formally
held to account, in the way that Adam Price suggests.

Here, in his own words, was what Adam Price suggested;
"Three centuries ago the Commons called impeachment 'the
chief institution for the preservation of the government.' It has
been a key weapon in the long struggle of parliament against the
abuse of executive power. It has been revived before, after long
periods of disuse, when the executive's hold on power-without-
responsibility seemed every bit as total as today," the Welsh member of Parliament declared on August 26, 2004. "Today a number
of MPs, including myself, are declaring our intention to bring a
Commons' motion of impeachment against the prime minister
in relation to the invasion of Iraq. This is the first time in more
than 150 years that such a motion has been brought against a
minister of the crown, and it is clearly not an undertaking we
enter into lightly. We do it with regret, but also with resolve. For
our first duty is to the people we represent, who feel they were
misled, whose trust was betrayed, who have been placed in harm's
way by the irresponsible actions of this prime minister. It is in
their name that we impeach him. It is in their name, and with all
the authority vested in us, that we implore him now to go."

Ten members of the House of Commons, including Johnson, joined Price that day in announcing their intention to impeach Blair for "high crimes and misdemeanours." Labour MP
Keith Vaz, a Blair loyalist, denounced the media for even covering
Price's initiative, dismissing it as "a silly story for the end of the
silly season." Blair's backers told reporters that impeachment was
"obsolete" in parliamentary terms. But Price pressed his case. "To
dust off Victorian constitutional histories and examine prece-

dents from the time of Charles I and Chaucer may seem bizarre,"
he said. "But the conduct of the prime minister has left people
and parliament with no alternative if we are to preserve the very
basis of democracy."

Price's arguments proved compelling to a surprising cross
section of parliamentarians. Eventually, he was joined by members of Plaid Cymru and the Scottish National Party, Conservatives and Liberal Democrats—war supporters and war foes,
right-wingers and left-wingers, former Cabinet ministers and
backbench outsiders—in pressing for parliamentary action. It
was an unprecedented assemblage, pulling together Douglas
Hogg, a minister in the cabinet of the former Tory prime minister Margaret Thatcher, and radical MP George Galloway, who no
one ever accused of being a Thatcherite. Missing were members
of Blair's Labour Party, even Peter Kilfoyle, the MP who had first
raised the impeachment question. Under threat of official sanction, even those Labour parliamentarians who had condemned
the war shied away from pursuing the grail of impeachment.

This was understandable in a political context, but indefensible in a moral one, explained Edward Garnier—a former Conservative Party spokesman on legal issues and a supporter of
the invasion when Blair proposed it—who described and dis-
dained the caution of his fellow members of the House of Commons in an interview with the *Financial Times*. "There are several
categories of members who will not support this," explained
Garnier. "The No 10 machinists will pour scorn on it. The political realists will say it won't work and that we should wait for
the next election, and the yawners—Pavlovian dogs who see no
purpose in being an MP except to be re-elected—won't even
think about the constitutional issue of holding the executive to

account. But there is nothing improper about requiring the prime minister to tell the truth to the House of Commons. Elective dictatorships begin when the commons gets lazy."

Garnier and his fellow Tory, Douglas Hogg, joined the leader of Plaid Cymru, Elfyn Llwyd, and the leader of the Scottish National Party, Alex Salmond, in drafting an impeachment motion during the fall, when the United States was wrapped up with the presidential contest between Bush and Democrat John Kerry. It was submitted for review the day before the U.S. election. Ten days later, legal advisers to the speaker of the Commons accepted the language of the motion—confirming beyond question that impeachment was not "obsolete"—and on November 24, 2004, the motion appeared on the official order paper of proposed parliamentary actions.

Simple and direct in its language, yet uncompromising in its message, the motion urged:

That a select committee of not more than 13 Members be appointed to investigate and to report to the House on the conduct of the Prime Minister in relation to the war against Iraq and in particular to consider;

(a) the conclusion of the Iraq Survey Group that in March 2003 Iraq did not possess weapons of mass destruction and had been essentially free of them since the mid 1990s

(b) the Prime Minister's acknowledgement that he was wrong when in and before March 2003 he asserted that Iraq was then in possession of chemical or biological weapons or was then en-

gaged in active efforts to develop nuclear
weapons or was thereby a current or serious
threat to the UK national interest or that possession of WMD then enabled Iraq to inflict real
damage upon the region and the stability of the
world

(c) the opinion of the Secretary General of the
United Nations that the invasion of Iraq in 2003
was unlawful

(d) whether there exist sufficient grounds to impeach the Rt Hon Tony Blair on charges of
gross misconduct in his advocacy of the case for
war against Iraq and in his conduct of policy in
connection with that war.

That the Committee shall within 48 days of its appointment report to this House such resolutions, articles
of impeachment or other recommendations as it shall
think fit.

Impeachment was again "a live instrument of the constitution." That did not mean, however, that the process was going
forward.

On the day the motion was filed, author Frederick Forsyth
appeared with other leading Brits to endorse the measure.
"When Blair swore to the nation that he had seen classified reports proving Saddam was armed to the teeth, he could not have
been telling the truth because the only people who could have
prepared and delivered such a document were the Secret Intelligence Service. And they didn't," declared Forsyth, a prominent

backer of the Conservative opposition. "As lying to the House is a resigning matter, and always has been, the Tory Party should now throw its unanimous weight behind the impeachment motion."

This did not happen. Just as Democratic leaders in the U.S. Congress initially shied away from supporting even an investigation of whether the actions of the Bush administration might merit impeachment—the most tepid initial step in the process—leaders of the main British opposition party officially urged its members of parliament not to sign the impeachment motion. Though eleven Tory MPs broke with their party to sign the motion, the vast majority did not. Thus, the motion lacked the critical mass to force immediate parliamentary action.

Yet it did force a public debate, drawing daily attention in the newspapers of the United Kingdom and on the broadcasts of the BBC to the fundamental question of Blair's suitability to remain in office, and inspiring investigations such as the one that unearthed the Downing Street notes. Each day, supporters of impeachment resubmitted their motion, and on March 17, 2005, as the second anniversary of the invasion of Iraq approached, Adam Price rose to address his colleagues. Reminding them that they had voted to authorize the invasion based on assurances from Blair, Price announced that "a motion of impeachment is before us."

"There is compelling evidence that the prime minister misled this house in taking us to war," the young parliamentarian continued. "Isn't it high time we held him to account?"

The speaker of the Commons, who was more loyal to Blair than to the tradition of an office once occupied by the most courageous challenger of the royal prerogative, Peter de la Mare, ordered Price to withdraw his remarks—on the grounds that they cast the prime minister in an unfair light. Price refused and was expelled from the Commons. That evening, the BBC carried dramatic footage of the Welshman exiting the chamber. To the gathered reporters, Price announced, "Most people now believe that the prime minister deliberately deceived Parliament and the people. He even deceived members of his own cabinet in taking us to war two years ago. But the rules of the game in Westminster mean we cannot say what most of us think. The prime minister misled us and MPs must be able to debate the issue. We will not let Tony Blair's lies and deceit be forgotten. 100,000 people have died in the course of this conflict. We must take a stand. I will not be gagged and Parliament should not allow itself to be silenced."

Less than two months later, Price was returned to Parliament with an increased majority by the voters of the Welsh valleys in an election that saw Blair's Labour Party suffer a six percent drop in support nationally and end the day with 101 fewer seats than it had secured in the previous national vote. Few doubted that the focus on questions of whether he had misled the nation into a bloody and protracted war did severe damage to the prime minister's credibility and his political appeal. Within hours of the vote, Robin Cook, a former foreign minister in Blair's cabinet, suggested that "the question Tony Blair should be reflecting on this weekend is . . . whether now might be a better time to let a new leader in who could then achieve the unity we need if we are going to go forward." Labour MP Glenda Jackson, the actress who had also served as one of Blair's ministers before becoming an outspoken critic of the Iraq war, was more direct: "The people have spoken," she wrote in the *Daily Mail* newspaper. "In fact they've screamed at the top of their lungs. And their message is clear. They want Tony Blair gone."

Blair was not impeached. But he was being held to account.

In a very real sense, this is the true genius of impeachment. The specific legislative process need not be completed for it to change history—as Richard Nixon's resignation from the presidency on the eve of his impeachment in 1974 proved. It can be stalled by partisan majorities loyal to an irresponsible leader and still extract a measure of accountability from him.

By the fall of 2005, one year after the impeachment motion was first submitted, Price was back in the news, declaring, "Too many questions remain unanswered about the way we were taken to war in Iraq, and we demand to have them answered. Neither the Hutton nor the Butler Inquiries addressed the central question—were the Parliament and country misled? Therefore it is essential that a committee is set up to investigate the matter thoroughly. If we do not restore proper accountability to the Government, it will corrupt our whole society by providing evidence that allows our enemies to call our democracy a sham." On November 23, 2005, he submitted a new motion, which declared: "This House believes that there should be a select committee of 7 Members, being members of her Majesty's Privy Council, to review the way in which the responsibilities of Government were discharged in relation to Iraq and all matters relevant thereto, in the period leading up to military action in that country in March 2003 and in its aftermath." This time, party leaders were unable to restrain their members. Within weeks, Price was joined by 150 members of parliament, representing every party, including Labour. To be sure, the call for an inquiry was not so blunt an instrument as the motion to impeach. But this, too, is the genius of impeachment. To speak of impeachment is radical. But to do so establishes in the minds of legislators and the people an understanding of the full consequence of the debate. It clears the thicket and opens the path of honest inquiry that is the essential element of accountability in a democracy.

To speak of impeachment, seriously and without flinching in the face of ridicule and political intriguing, renews and invigorates not just the processes that hold leaders to account, but the language that is used to do so. This was the case when General Sir Michael Rose, a decorated British military commander who led the United Nations mission in Bosnia, was asked by the BBC about Blair's statements and actions prior to the invasion of Iraq. Rose replied, "The politics was wrong, that he rarely declared what his ultimate aims were, as far as we can see, in terms of harping continually on weapons of mass destruction when actually he probably had some other strategy in mind. And secondly, the consequences of that war have been quite disastrous both for the people of Iraq and also for the west in terms of our wider interests in the war against global terror."

"To go to war on what turns out to be false grounds is something that no one should be allowed to walk away from," he continued. "I think the politicians should be held to account . . . my view is that Blair should be impeached."

Impeachment would be about more than punishing Blair, the general concluded. Holding a prime minister to account in a particular moment would set a precedent that might not soon be forgotten. "That," Sir Michael declared, "would prevent the politicians treating quite so carelessly the subject of taking a country into war."

James R. Mann

"He is subject to the rule of law and to justice, and in my role under my oath, he will get it, be he president or pauper."

CHAPTER 3

DESPOTS, DEMOCRATS AND THE NECESSITY OF A DISSENTING OPPOSITION

I am fully aware that many American people consider that the President is being attacked by sinister forces in this country, by the left-wing press or by the Democrats, and I can assure this gentleman that it matters not to me his party or his position. He is subject to the rule of law and to justice, and in my role under my oath, he will get it, be he President or be he pauper.

South Carolina Democrat
James Mann, 1974, explaining his
support for the impeachment of
Richard Nixon

"Impeachment" is, necessarily and appropriately, an unsettling term when uttered in the presence of an abusive president or the aides who are charged—as were the royal retainers of old—with maintaining the sovereign's uncontested power. Only the most noble of imperial executives, or the most disgusted of appointees, could find comfort in the promise—or, more precisely, the threat—of accountability.

So it has ever been, so it shall ever be.

But, too frequently in contemporary America, "impeachment" has also proven to be an unsettling word when uttered in the presence of the leaders of the congressional opposition to a president who has abused his powers. That is not as it should be. With a few rare exceptions—such as the 1868 impeachment by Radical Republicans of President Andrew Johnson, a Democrat who had allied with the Republicans to run on Abraham Lincoln's 1864 ticket, and the attempted impeachment of Republican president Herbert Hoover in 1932 by renegade Republican representative Louis T. McFadden—history tells us that it is the congressional opposition, motivated by the imprecise mix of partisanship and sincere concern for the nation that has always been essential to making change in a democracy, that dares propose opening the procedural cabinet and pulling out what Lord Bryce referred to as "the heroic medicine" of impeachment.

Partisanship ought never to be the sole, nor even primary, motivation for the impeachment of a president. And when it is, as was seen with the Whig-sponsored impeachments and censure motions of several presidents in the 1840s and with the Republican-led impeachment of Bill Clinton in the late 1990s, the initiative tends to collapse before achieving its ends. But, even in these extreme cases, it would be wrong to dismiss the partisan impulse as a wholly illegitimate motivation, particularly in the critical initial stages of an impeachment debate. After all, if the point of impeachment is to hold the executive branch to a standard of accountability, the members of Congress who are most likely to recognize abuses against that standard are almost always those who, for reasons of ideology or simple competitiveness, are inclined to be skeptical of the current occupant of the Oval Office.

That's the logic of politics. And, for the most part, it serves as a useful counterbalance to the penchant of congressional members of the president's own party to cut him as much slack as the mood of the moment will allow.

Unfortunately, in the contemporary moment, when the point and the promise of impeachment is so little understood by politicians and pundits, political pragmatism often trumps the healthy partisan impulse to challenge an executive whose administration has spun out of control. Opposition leaders, worried about appearing too aggressive in their affronts to a president of the competing party, back away from the battlements. They counsel caution, suggesting that it is "wiser" to wait until an election when, if their thinly veiled hopes are realized, power will be handed to them by frustrated and fearful voters.

The problem with this equation, of course, is that it robs the process of the dynamism that is essential to checking and balancing the executive branch. An opposition party that "waits for the next election" is not being bipartisan, it is being politically strategic. It is not doing what's right for the country, it is doing what's right for itself—or, more precisely, what leaders who are disinclined to take risks think is politically "wise." This failure of will serves to strengthen the executive, both in the long term and, frequently, in a short term that proves electorally disadvantageous to the opposition party trying so hard to avoid the appearance of being "too partisan" that it ultimately fails to appear to be a credible alternative. When congressional Democrats failed to pursue impeachment as the necessary response to the Iran-Contra revelations of rampant illegality in the Reagan White House—rejecting the advice of Henry B. González, the wily Texas congressman who alone introduced the appropriate articles in 1987—they thought they were positioning the party for victory in the coming presidential election. Instead, Vice President George Herbert Walker Bush, having recovered from the gentle slap on the wrist he received from Congress for his own involvement in the scandal, was elected to the presidency in 1988 by a landslide and expected Democratic advances in Congress failed to materialize.

Pulling punches in a political battle usually results in a knockout, with the party that holds back collapsing to the mat and struggling, often for a very long time, to finally get up again. And the Democratic Party of the George Herbert Walker Bush years, with its inexplicable penchant for pulling punches, runs the very real risk of being flattened not once but repeatedly if it fails to confront the issue of rampant wrongdoing on the part of the Bush administration.

That is certainly the message that is coming from the grass roots of the party, where frustrated activists began in 2005 to talk about impeachment with a gusto and a gumption that was rarely evident in the precincts occupied by their party's Washington "leaders."

In the spring of 2005, barely a month after the Downing Street Memo revealed that aides to British prime minister Tony Blair believed the Bush administration was "fixing" intelligence to make the case for war with Iraq, the Wisconsin Democratic Party held its annual convention. Hundreds of the party faithful made their way from around the Midwestern state to the university town of Oshkosh for a weekend of pep talking, partying and resolving.

A surprise resolution that weekend was inspired by the revelations from Britain. It proposed the impeachment of key members of the Bush administration for high crimes and misdemeanors.

Advanced by rural and small-town party stalwarts like Buzz Davis, a retiree who started a group called the Stoughton Area Democrats in his south-central Wisconsin hometown—

Stoughton, population 12,354, has been a hotbed of antiwar sentiment going back to World War I, when voters there were big backers of U.S. senator Robert M. La Follette—the resolution was an expression of righteous indignation over evidence that the administration had deceived the American people and their Congress in order to promote a war of whim.

Written as a call on Congress, it read:

> WHEREAS, the Downing Street Memo shows that Bush, Cheney and Rumsfeld began planning and executing the war on Iraq before seeking Congressional and UN approval;
>
> WHEREAS, UN weapons inspectors showed prior to the invasion that there were no weapons of mass destruction in Iraq; and
>
> WHEREAS, there is further mounting evidence that the Administration lied or misled about "mushroom clouds," "connections to 9/11," and "war as a last resort" as they sought UN, Congressional, and public approvals;
>
> THEREFORE, RESOLVED, the Democratic Party of Wisconsin asks Congress to immediately begin impeachment proceedings against President Bush, Vice President Cheney and Defense Secretary Rumsfeld.

Without any advance preparation, without any aggressive lobbying or tortured debate, the convention voted with little or no opposition to endorse impeachment.

The Wisconsin Democrats were not radicals who, in their determination to blow up the Bush administration, were willing to commit political suicide. They were, for the most part, veteran party activists who had worked hard trying to win the White House back from the Republicans in 2004 and who were determined to work even harder to replace Bush with a Democrat in 2008. They were grandmothers wearing knitted sweaters, retired state employees in sports jackets, union representatives in T-shirts and young moms drawn into the party by Howard Dean's presidential campaign of the previous year. They did not fear that endorsing impeachment would cost them congressional seats or the White House. And they were not alone. State Democratic parties from New Mexico to Nevada to North Carolina to California and Maine would, by the spring of 2006, endorse impeachment, as would local party groups across the country.

Why were state party activists so quick to embrace impeachment at a time when their party's leaders in Washington were, for the most part, terrified by the thought of doing so? It had a lot to do with the proximity of the activists to the party's grassroots base. Polling suggested as early as the fall of 2005 that the great mass of self-identified Democrats had grown comfortable with impeachment. Actually, "comfortable" was the wrong word. In much of the country, the accurate term was "enthusiastic."

A Zogby International poll conducted around the time of the Wisconsin convention asked likely voters nationwide: "Do you agree or disagree that, if President Bush did not tell the truth about his reasons for going to war with Iraq, Congress should hold him accountable through impeachment?" Among all voters, the split was 50 percent to 42 percent against impeachment, but Democrats favored impeachment under the circumstances described by a margin of 59 percent to 30 percent. In November of 2005, when Zogby again asked the question, support for impeachment had risen, with the split among all voters shifting to

53 percent in favor of holding Bush to account if he had lied and 42 percent opposed. Among Democrats, a striking 76 percent backed impeachment.

After it was revealed in December of 2005 that the president had authorized the NSA to conduct warrantless wiretaps on the phone conversations of Americans, Zogby asked: "If President Bush wiretapped American citizens without the approval of a judge, do you agree or disagree that Congress should consider holding him accountable through impeachment?" Overall, 52 percent of those surveyed agreed, while 43 percent disagreed. Among Democrats, 66 percent agreed. In the battleground state of Pennsylvania, a separate poll by Zogby, which was commissioned by the political website OpEdNews.com, asked Democrats whether they would be likely to vote for a congressional candidate who "supports having impeachment proceedings against President Bush." Eighty-five percent of those surveyed said they would be likely to support such a candidate, while only 7 percent said they would be unlikely to do so.

Yet, for the most part, national Democratic leaders rejected even the gentlest talk of officially sanctioning President Bush and Vice President Cheney in much the same manner that a vampire rejects the Host. Even when they were offered clear evidence that the communities they represented were overwhelmingly in favor of action, Democratic congressional leaders explicitly rejected it. A classic case study came in early 2006, when San Francisco's Board of Supervisors voted 7–3 for Democratic supervisor Chris Daly's resolution urging California's congressional representatives to pursue impeachment of Bush and Cheney. The bill of particulars discussed by Daly and other supervisors echoed concerns raised by U.S. representative John Conyers, the ranking

Democrat on the House Judiciary Committee, and the several dozen Democratic House members who had already cosponsored Conyers' call for the creation of a select committee to investigate administration preparations for war with Iraq before obtaining congressional authorization, manipulation of prewar intelligence, encouragement and countenancing of torture and retaliation against critics—and to make recommendations regarding grounds for possible impeachment.

While a number of Bay Area representatives were among the cosponsors of the Conyers resolution—including congressional Progressive Caucus cochairs Barbara Lee and Lynn Woolsey—the most powerful member of the House from the region, and the primary representative of the city of San Francisco, was not on board. Indeed, House Minority Leader Nancy Pelosi proved to be almost as frightened by the word "impeachment" as the right-wing talk radio hosts who doth protest too much whenever the term is mentioned.

Pelosi was confronted at a January 2006 town hall meeting in San Francisco by constituents who detailed administration misdeeds and chanted: "Impeach! Impeach!" Her response, according to a *San Francisco Bay Guardian* report, was initially a political one: "For those of you concerned about these issues, I urge you to channel your energies into the 2006 elections," she told the crowd.

Pressed on whether she would join senior Democrats in the California delegation—such as Pete Stark and Maxine Waters—in backing the House resolution to investigate matters related to impeachment, Pelosi answered, "I do not intend to support Mr. Conyers's resolution."

Seeking to quiet the ensuing chorus of boos, Pelosi said, "We have a responsibility to try to bring this country together."

According to the *Guardian* report, one of the San Franciscans in the audience shouted back, "You have a responsibility to uphold the Constitution!"

In a matter of weeks, that response was no longer just a shout from the crowd. Impeachment had been endorsed by the board of supervisors of the city Pelosi represented in Congress. Yet, as MSNBC national affairs writer Tom Curry reported after the San Francisco vote, the minority leader continued to do everything in her power to undermine discussion of the issue. "Censure President Bush? Impeach him? Or discreetly kill those ideas to avoid fueling Republican intensity?" Curry wrote. "House Democratic Leader Nancy Pelosi has chosen the 'discreetly kill' option, arguing that the current impeachment/censure talk is just a pointless distraction from the party's message." "I think that we should solve this issue electorally," Pelosi repeatedly argued, conveniently avoiding mention of the fact that—like Andrew Johnson when he was impeached in 1868, like Harry Truman when Republicans discussed impeaching him in 1952, like Richard Nixon when the House Judiciary Committee voted to impeach him in 1974, and like Bill Clinton when he was impeached in 1998—George Bush and Dick Cheney were unlikely ever again to face the American electorate.

While Pelosi obviously feared that the very mention of impeachment might draw otherwise disengaged Republicans to the polls, Curry quoted a grassroots Democrat who suggested that Pelosi had miscalculated. "The Democratic base is getting sick and tired of the whining, wimpy Democratic leadership at the national level," explained Darla Wilshire, of Altoona, Pennsylvania. "We are the voters who will stay home in November, not the Republicans. Why? Because the party can't stand up for its principles . . ."

The aversion even to talk of impeachment—let alone to action—on the part of so many congressional Democrats, despite their own acknowledgments that members of the administration had broken laws, lied and contravened the system of checks and balances mandated by the Constitution, reflected a broader disconnect between party "leaders" and the party's base. Not since the dying Whig Party of the early 1850s, which could not bring itself to call once and for all for the abolition of slavery, has the national leadership of an opposition party been so fully delinked from the passions of the voters on whom it relies to remain politically competitive.

The disconnect was thrown into stark relief in March 2006, when maverick Democratic U.S. senator Russ Feingold asked the Senate to officially censure President Bush for breaking the law by authorizing an illegal wiretapping program and for misleading Congress and the American people about the existence and legality of that program. Charging that the wiretapping program was in direct violation of the Foreign Intelligence Surveillance Act (FISA)—which makes it a crime to wiretap Americans in the United States without a warrant or a court order—Feingold argued that Congress could not avoid facing the fact that fundamental constitutional issues were at stake.

"The President must be held accountable for authorizing a program that clearly violates the law and then misleading the country about its existence and its legality," explained the progressive Democrat from Wisconsin. "The President's actions, as well as his misleading statements to both Congress and the public about the program, demand a serious response. If Congress does not censure the President, we will be tacitly condoning his actions, and undermining both the separation of powers and the rule of law."

There was never any question that Feingold's motion faced an uphill fight in a Republican-controlled Senate that did not appear to be inclined to make Bush the first president since Andrew Jackson to be officially censured by a house of Congress. But the initiative raised the stakes at a point when the Wisconsin senator and civil libertarians had grown frustrated with the failure of Congress to aggressively challenge the administration's penchant for warrantless wiretapping.

Republican senators were proposing to rewrite laws in order to remove at least some of the barriers to eavesdropping, arguing that the president needed flexibility to pursue his war on terror. But Feingold rejected the suggestion that changing the rules after the fact would absolve the president. "This issue is not about whether the government should be wiretapping terrorists—of course it should, and it can under current law," the senator said. "But this President and this administration decided to break the law and they have yet to give a convincing explanation of why their actions were necessary, appropriate, or legal. Passing more laws will not change the fact that the President broke the ones already in place and for that, Congress must hold him accountable."

Feingold had chosen to propose censure because he wanted to give Congress an option short of impeachment for sanctioning Bush.

Though the censure procedure is not outlined in the Constitution—as is impeachment—it is well established in the history and traditions of the Congress. Andrew Jackson was censured in 1834 for refusing to cooperate with a congressional investigation, and there have been many moves over the years to use the procedure to hold presidents to account. In 1998, the then-new online activist group, MoveOn.org, proposed that as an alternative to impeaching Bill Clinton for lying to a grand jury and obstructing justice, the president could be censured. After rejecting impeachment in 1999, senators discussed censuring Clinton but failed to muster the votes to do so. And, in addition to his December 2005 resolution calling for the establishment of a select committee to make recommendations regarding impeachment, Conyers had introduced separate resolutions to censure President Bush and Vice President Cheney for refusing to cooperate with congressional investigations into the manipulation and mismanagement of intelligence by the administration when it was lobbying the House and Senate to authorize and support the invasion of Iraq.

While the impeachment process can lead to the removal of a president or vice president from office, a vote to censure merely condemns the offending official. Censure is best understood as a flexing of muscle by the legislative branch, a signal that the executive needs to either acknowledge and correct an inappropriate course of action or face more serious sanction.

Though Feingold suggested that the president's authorization of warrantless wiretapping was "in the strike zone" of meeting the standard of an impeachable offense, he was offering the Senate an easy out. "The president has broken the law and, in some way, he must be held accountable," explained the senator, who even his critics recognize as one of the Capitol's ablest legal minds. "Congress has to reassert our system of government, and the cleanest and the most efficient way to do that is to censure the president."

The White House did not respond immediately to Feingold's announcement. But Republican senators rallied to the administration's defense in predictable lockstep fashion. Senate Majority Leader Bill Frist, R-Tennessee, dismissed the censure proposal as "a crazy political move" that would weaken the president's hand in a time of war. U.S. senator John Warner, R-Virginia, accused Feingold of "political grandstanding."

Feingold's record of challenging the misdeeds of both Democratic and Republican administrations made those charges a tough sell. The ranking Democrat on the Constitution subcommittee of the Senate Judiciary Committee, he had repeatedly clashed with the Bush administration, and before that with the Clinton administration, over separation of powers issues. Indeed, Feingold was the only Democrat who broke party ranks in 1999 to oppose a proposal to dismiss charges against Clinton before the Senate trial on the articles of impeachment against the Democratic president had been completed. An outspoken civil libertarian, the Wisconsin Democrat had a long record of confronting abuses of constitutional protections by the executive branch. He also had a skill for putting accountability issues in proper political perspective.

When it was first revealed that, despite previous denials by the president and his aides, Bush had repeatedly authorized a secret program by the National Security Agency to listen in on the phone calls of Americans, Feingold responded with the seminal statement of the era: "We have a system of law. [Bush] just can't make up the law. It would turn George Bush not into President George Bush, but King George Bush."

With his reverence for the Constitution and the intents of the founders and with his own track record, Feingold offered Democrats a credible message and also a credible messenger. Yet, fearing the politics of impeachment, they rejected both.

It was a classic political misstep.

That Feingold was counseling a wise course of action for an

opposition party in a time of constitutional crisis should have been immediately evident to his fellow Democrats. But if they still needed confirmation, they got it quickly—and from a dramatic, if not unexpected, source.

Feingold's censure call incurred the wrath of the uncontested champion of executive excess, Dick Cheney.

Dismissing Feingold's proposal as "outrageous," the vice president told a crowd in the senator's home state within hours after the censure issue was raised that Americans want to be spied on secretly. Rejecting the suggestion that citizens might be concerned about the administration's admitted violations of laws designed to preserve and protect the constitutionally-defined right of Americans to be secure from secret searches and seizures, Cheney said, "The American people have already made their decision and they agree with the president."

This is an old dodge in debates about censure and impeachment. Allies of the offending official claim that any act by a president or his aides during a term to which that president has been elected were approved by the voters at the time of the balloting. These blanket claims of popular absolution are intended to portray calls for accountability as antidemocratic. Yet they invariably rest on a premise that is itself antithetical to American democracy as it was established and intended to function—since the proponents of this line imagine that each presidential election produces a "king for four years," precisely the state of affairs that the founders most feared.

Just as invariably, these claims lack a basis in the facts of the particular elections that are cited as validation for any and all abuses by the executives in question.

In the case of Cheney's attack on Feingold's censure motion, for instance, the vice president knew full well that he was claiming a false mandate. The warrantless wiretapping initiative had been kept completely secret before the 2004 presidential election—by the White House and by the *New York Times* newspaper, which apparently had the story that fall but chose not to report it until more than a year later. Voters never were given an opportunity to decide whether they wanted to reelect a president who first lied to them about spying and then, when caught, brazenly declared that he would continue to contravene the Constitution and authorize illegal eavesdropping on the phone conversations of U.S. citizens.

At the most basic level, Cheney was being disingenuous about the issue of whether the administration's wiretapping regime had public approval.

Yet he was not being disingenuous about his belief that congressional challenges to the authority of his—or, presumably, any other—administration to do whatever it wants should be dismissed as "outrageous." Since his days as an aide to then-president Richard Nixon, Cheney had been a militant proponent of expanding the powers of the executive branch. As a representative from Wyoming, he led congressional opposition to holding the Reagan administration to account for the lawlessness exposed in the Iran-Contra scandal; as secretary of defense he counseled the first President Bush that he did not need congressional approval to launch the Gulf War of 1991; and from his first hours as the second President Bush's vice president he had exhibited fierce disdain for Congress in general and, in particular, for the oversight responsibilities afforded the House and Senate under the Constitution.

While Cheney was entirely sincere in his disregard for Fein-

gold's censure motion, the same could not be said of Senate
Democrats, the vast majority of whom shied away from signing
on for reasons that can only be described as hypocritical.

There's no question that most, if not all, Senate Democrats
believed by the spring of 2006 that the president had violated the
Foreign Intelligence Surveillance Act when he directed the National Security Agency to begin listening in on the phone conversations of Americans without going through the simple
process of obtaining the appropriate warrants. Yet only California
Democrat Barbara Boxer and Iowa Democrat Tom Harkin were
quick to endorse Feingold's censure motion. The Wisconsin senator also got a crumb from John Kerry, the Democratic party's
2004 presidential nominee, who said he was "interested" in the
resolution because "the president ought to be held accountable,
and I think he broke the law."

But most of Feingold's fellow partisans went out of their way
to avoid even discussing the resolution.

While a maverick Republican, Rhode Island moderate
Lincoln Chafee, hailed the censure motion as a "positive" vehicle
for promoting debate about constitutional concerns that had
been raised by the Bush administration's civil-liberties-be-
damned pursuit of the the war on terror, the majority of Democratic senators refused to comment directly on the move to
sanction the president. And several, led by Connecticut's Joe
Lieberman, announced that they preferred to work with Republicans to construct cover for the administration's past illegality by
rewriting the rules regarding the initiation of surveillance programs.

The line that was peddled quietly by a number of the senators, and somewhat more loudly by many pundits—when they
weren't accusing Feingold of positioning himself for a 2008 pres-

idential run, as if that somehow sapped his initiative of legitimacy—was that it was the wrong time for congressional Democrats to develop a spine. With Bush and Cheney's poll ratings falling to record lows, and with indications that Americans might be ready for change, Democratic insiders were afraid to do anything that could upset their chances in the November 2006 elections. The fear was that being "too tough" on Bush—by, say, suggesting that the administration must abide by the law—would make Democrats appear shrill and cost the party's candidates votes in the fall.

Apart from the fact that White House political czar Karl Rove's spin machine would label the Democrats "shrill"—not to mention "unpatriotic" and "dangerous" in a "time of war"—for simply suggesting that voters might want to switch control of the House and Senate out of the hands of the president's party, the arguments against censure put the Democrats right back in the corner where they had found themselves again and again since Bush and Cheney took office.

The opposition party that too rarely opposed appeared once more to stand for nothing. There did not seem to be any principle, not even respect for the rule of law, that motivated most Democratic party leaders. As such, their party came off as an election machine that would compromise on anything and everything in order to win in November. That created an opening for Republicans who had argued time and again, with considerable success, that Bush, Cheney and their congressional allies might not always get things right but at least they operated from a place of conviction—particularly on matters of national security.

The failure to embrace Feingold's censure motion highlights the crisis that befalls any opposition party that takes the related options of censure and impeachment off the table. When an opposition party fails to function as such, it harms not just itself but the country. And the recent history of the Democratic party is nothing if not a record of failure. The party has, at too many critical junctures in the early years of the twenty-first century, refused to function as a check or a balance to Republican hegemony—much as the Republican party failed to check or balance Democratic hegemony at critical junctions in the mid to late twentieth century.

Such failures invariably leave fundamental questions unasked, and fundamental steps untaken. And, in the context of President Bush's second term, they do not bode well for any movement to reintroduce the standard that no man, be he king or president, stands above the law.

Yet, as the polling suggests, such a movement is precisely what Democrats in particular and Americans in general demand if the evidence of wrongdoing has been produced. As has so frequently been the case across history, the people are more comfortable with impeachment than the powerful.

With calls for accountability from the grass roots growing louder in the first months of 2006, as state parties, city councils and town meetings around the country penned their own articles of impeachment, Democratic-leaning pundits rushed in to restrain the rebellion. Yes, yes, the response came, of course Bush is a lawbreaker. Yes, yes, of course he should be impeached. But, no, no, don't mention the word—not with an election coming.

Author and agitator Arianna Huffington summed up the sentiment in a February 2006 column titled "You Want to Discuss Impeachment? Give Me a Call on Nov. 8th."

"Does Bush deserve to be impeached? Absolutely," wrote Huffington. "So should Democrats rally around nascent efforts to impeach the president? Absolutely not!"

Noting that the case for impeachment—on the grounds of lying to Congress in the run up to the invasion of Iraq, torture scandals and the rank illegality of the warrantless wiretapping program—had been well made by former U.S. representative Elizabeth Holtzman, the member of the Watergate-era House Judiciary Committee who had begun writing on the subject, Huffington argued,

> Nevertheless, a push to impeach would be nothing but a huge—and pointless—distraction.
>
> [The] House is controlled by the GOP and the votes are simply not there to impeach. Instead, the effort would just take up precious oxygen, energy, and passion better used demonstrating to the American public that the president and his party have made us less safe as a country," she explained. "This is the case Democrats need to be making: Bush's imperial adventure in Iraq has had devastating consequences on the real battle at hand—keeping us safe and secure . . . Election Day 2006 is just eight months away. The best way to hold President Bush accountable for abusing his power is to vote his fellow Republicans out of office and give control of Congress (including the Judiciary Committee) back to the Democrats. We need to do everything in our power to make that happen. If we succeed, give me a call on November 8th—maybe then we can talk about impeachment.

Huffington's line was echoed by the equally progressive and usually thoughtful Harold Meyerson, who, several days later, wrote an amusing column for the *Washington Post* in which he urged his ninety-two-year-old mother, Estelle, to clam up about impeachment. "At her house one afternoon, talking on the phone, I reached for a pad of paper to jot down some notes and found her handwritten agenda for the day. There was a list of vegetables. Then it said, 'Cola-Cola.' Then it said, 'Impeach Bush.' Underlined," recalled Meyerson, who bemoaned the fact that his mom was no longer alone in "preaching the gospel of impeachment."

"It's all over the blogosphere," an agitated Meyerson explained. "It's the cover story in the current *Harper's*. The San Francisco Board of Supervisors has passed an impeachment resolution. Antiwar activists, civil libertarians, all the usual-suspect constituencies have growing impeachment tendencies. But it's reaching beyond the usual suspects, as I discovered last month when I appeared on a media panel before the national legislative conference of a major union. Local activists from across the nation spent an hour asking us questions, and one out of every three queries, it seemed to me, boiled down to, 'How can we impeach this guy?' "

Meyerson's answer was "we can't"—not because Bush is beyond reproach but because "to dwell on impeachment now would be to drain energy from the election efforts that need to succeed if impeachment is ever truly to be on the agenda."

So the counsel from Meyerson, one of the savvier political writers on the left, was to try a bait-and-switch. Run on health care and education, win the Congress and then, perhaps, begin to entertain questions of impeachment. The problem with such strategies is twofold: First, they misread the politics of impeachment. Second, they make impeachment nothing more than a partisan political act—precisely what House Minority Whip

Leslie Arends, an Illinois Republican, termed it in 1974 when, on
the eve of the House Judiciary Committee vote on articles of impeachment against Richard Nixon, he declared, "Impeachment is
purely a Democratic maneuver. We ought to recognize it as such
and we ought to stand up as Republicans and oppose the whole
scheme." Within days, Arends looked very much the fool, as more
than a third of the Judiciary Committee's Republican members,
including several key conservatives, cast votes in favor of impeachment. Within weeks, Arends no longer looked but indeed
was the fool, as voters swept from office dozens of Republicans
who had opposed impeachment and reduced membership in
Arends' caucus to 144—less than one-third of the entire House.
In Senate races that year, three anti-impeachment Republican
incumbents were defeated, while open seats in the traditionally
Republican states of Vermont and New Hampshire fell to the
Democrats.

Those results provided an immediate and seemingly conclu-
sive counter to the claim, made at the time by Senate Minority
Leader Hugh Scott, R-Pennsylvania, that "history does not deal
gently with regicides." In fact, the opposite has generally been
true. The popular appeal of removing royals—go they by the designation of "king" or "president"—has always been more substantial than the political class would prefer to acknowledge. One
year after members of the Whig Party, led by former president
John Quincy Adams, unsuccessfully attempted to impeach President John Tyler, the Whigs picked up seven seats in the House—
increasing the size of their caucus by 10 percent—while Tyler
exited politics. Just weeks after he lobbied for the impeachment
of Andrew Johnson in 1868, Ulysses S. Grant won the Republican nomination for the presidency, and he then prevailed by a

landslide that fall. After raising the issue of impeaching President Harry Truman for seizing control of the nation's steel plants in 1952, Republicans won the presidency and gained two seats in the Senate and twenty-two in the House. Even in 1998, as congressional Republicans prepared to impeach President Clinton on charges that, polls showed, most Americans thought were motivated more by partisanship and personal scorn than concern for the rule of law, both the House and Senate remained safely in GOP hands. The Senate saw no shift in the 55–45 majority Republicans held prior to the election, while the House saw a five-seat loss for the Republicans—one of the smaller shifts away from a majority party in the history of the country. Still, the 1998 election has entered into popular mythology as proof positive that impeachment is a dark science in which ambitious politicians engage at their peril.

Many of the same Democrats who dismissed the Republican push to impeach Clinton as illegitimate—Pelosi referred to the initiative as a "hatchet job on the presidency" that, she said, was inspired not by necessity but by the fact that "Republicans in the House are paralyzed with hatred of President Clinton"—took away from that exercise the "lesson" that they are now precluded from the legitimate exercise of their responsibilities by a new set of political rules that guarantees the punishment of any opposition party that seeks to hold a president to account. What this tortured political calculus fails to recognize is that, in the "impeachment election" of 1998, Republicans actually won a slightly higher percentage of the popular vote nationally for House seats than they had two years earlier—up from 47.8 in 1996 to 48 percent on the eve of the House Judiciary Committee hearings on Clinton's alleged crimes. The percentage of the vote nationally that went to Democratic House candidates fell from 48.1 in 1996 to 47.1 in 1998. Even more notable is the fact that Republicans whose names were closely associated with the impeachment push, such as House Judiciary Committee chair Henry Hyde, Wisconsin's James Sensenbrenner, California's James Rogan and Georgia's Bob Barr maintained past levels of support or, in the cases of Hyde and Sensenbrenner, improved their positions. To be sure, House Speaker Newt Gingrich's bumbling approach to the issue—as well as to his own personal affairs—led his caucus to pressure him to step down. But Hyde, Sensenbrenner and many of the other Republicans who were outspoken in their condemnation of Clinton remained leaders within their party and the House, control of which never shifted from Republican hands.

Whether the party controls the House, as did Democratic advocates for the impeachment of Nixon in 1974 or Republican advocates for the impeachment of Clinton in 1998, or whether it is competing for control of the House, as were Republicans who talked of impeaching Harry Truman in 1952, the notion that impeachment is "bad politics" for an opposition party is not grounded in reality. Rather, it is grounded in the ahistoric and hyperstrategic politics of a contemporary status quo that seeks to keep both political parties operating within the narrow boundaries that prevent surprises for entrenched officials, wealthy campaign contributors and powerful lobbyists. As long as impeachment is portrayed as the political third rail, standards of accountability remain low and prospects for a genuine course correction are diminished. The minority party that covets power is tempered in its approach, as are freethinkers within the majority party.

This absurd argument for maintaining a corrupt and dysfunctional status quo is, as always, attributed to popular will. The reliable line of defense for the neglect of constitutionally-defined duties is the claim that the American people are so horrified by the prospect of impeachment that they will smite any and all who raise it. But, as *Time* magazine noted when the House Judiciary Committee vote on the articles of impeachment against Nixon was approaching in the summer of 1974, even Republicans—after consulting constituents they had expected to be rabidly opposed to sanctioning the president but who, in fact, turned out to be fully supportive of accountability—were coming to the conclusion that "a vote for impeachment may be good politics."

In 1974, a vote for impeachment was especially good politics for members of the president's party, because getting on the right side of the wave of resentment toward Nixon could make the difference between political survival and defeat. But impeachment is almost always good politics for an opposition party—particularly an opposition party that is struggling to define itself.

Impeachment is good politics for a party in such a circumstance precisely because it is volatile. There are risks involved. Things have to be done right. That means that impeachment cannot be a mere partisan game. Raising the specter of the removal of a president or vice president brings with it a basic requirement that the opposition party make a case sufficient to convince not merely its own members but the greater mass of Americans—including the wavering adherents of the president's own party—that high crimes and misdemeanors have been committed and that the guilty must be called to account. It is a given that the case for impeachment must be grounded in arguments that are both rational and consequential. Even then, charges of partisanship will be leveled, as they always have been. It is point-less for the proponents of impeachment to take offense, and ridiculous for them to moan about how the political moment has required so "painful" and "undesirable" a step. Such talk, by its na-ture, suggests hypocrisy and calculation on the part of an opposi-tion party that will always face at least some suspicion that it acts in its own interest.

The counter to charges from defenders of an embattled ex-ecutive that impeachment is being pursued for partisan purposes comes not in a new set of talking points but in the dawning recognition on the part of the political class and the broader pop-ulation that a presidency has gone awry, and in the quality of the arguments for acting upon that recognition.

It is the understanding of this equation that gives an opposi-tion party, even one that may not form a congressional majority, its strength in a debate, no matter how formal or informal, over impeachment. As former South Carolina Democratic congress-man James Mann, the wily southern lawyer who emerged as an unexpectedly effective advocate for the removal of President Nixon, told the Judiciary Committee in the summer of 1974, "I am fully aware that many American people consider that the President is being attacked by sinister forces in this country, by the left-wing press or by the Democrats, and I can assure this gentleman that it matters not to me his party or his position. He is subject to the rule of law and to justice, and in my role under my oath, he will get it, be he President or be he pauper."

The benefit of an impeachment fight to an opposition party comes not in the removal of an individual who happens to wear the label of another party—since, under the current system, that individual is all but certain to be replaced by a partisan ally—but in the elevation of the discourse to a higher ground where politicians and voters can ponder the deeper meaning of democracy and the republican endeavor. It is in the confident occupation of that higher ground that an opposition party begins to look and sound like an appropriate guardian of the most cherished values and ideals of the nation.

By forging convincing arguments for impeachment, an opposition party—and sometimes the reforming wing of an offending president's own party—asserts itself as something more than the political equivalent of a sports team competing for a title. The bold gesture of declaring that a member of the executive branch of the government has transgressed so aggressively and so completely against his oath of office and his defined duties that he must be removed from office before the conclusion of his elected term has the potential to transform a previously listless and disengaged party into a political force that speaks what Walt Whitman referred to as "the pass-word primeval," that gives "the sign of democracy." When the whole of a political party finally concludes that it must take up the weighty responsibility of impeaching a president, as Democrats did in 1974 but Republicans never fully did in 1998, its language is clarified and transfigured. What Whitman referred to as "long dumb voices" are suddenly transformed into clarion calls, as a dialogue of governmental marginalia gives way to discussion of the intent of the founders, the duty of the people's representatives and the renewal of the republic.

When a political party speaks well and wisely of impeachment, frustrated voters come to see that party in a new way. It is no longer merely the tribune of its own ambition. It becomes a champion of the American experiment. To be sure, such a leap entails risk. But it is the risk-averse political party that is most likely to become the permanent opposition. There is no history, nor any rational impulse, that suggests the politics of caution and compromise are likely to bring the sort of political realignment that breaks the status quo and gives an opposition party not a temporary majority but the power to affect meaningful change in its own circumstance and that of the nation. This is the fundamental American understanding. This is the requirement of politics, not as the game that is played by so many contemporary retainers of both major parties, but as the essential struggle in which the founders engaged. Before either of the antecedents of the Democratic and Republican parties began to take shape, before the Federalists and the Anti-Federalists assembled their forces, the politics of what would become the United States was defined by another party—a party of revolution against the royal prerogative, the divine right of kings and the corruptions of empire associated with an essentially unfettered monarch.

It is never easy to reconnect with that revolutionary spirit, and the task cannot be accomplished in a halfhearted or insincere manner. But for a Democratic party that has yet to effectively identify itself as a force for the twenty-first century, there is much to be learned from the language and the passions of the eighteenth century. To speak without flinching, and without apology, about the rule of law, and about the duty of the legislative branch to hold the executive to account, is not a civics lesson. It is a return to the essential discussion of the nation. The values that underpin that discussion are permanent, to be sure, but their salience in any particular era is determined by the willingness of individual political players and parties to embrace them—and the effectiveness with which they do so. Thus, if Democrats hope to build a new and more vital relationship with the American people, a relationship that runs deeper than any particular issue or individual, leaders of the party must overcome the fear of impeachment that has so paralyzed them as an opposition force. This will only happen if they stop waiting for the next election to be bold, if they stop thinking, "If only we can attain a narrow majority in the House or Senate, all will be well." America needs an opposition party, not to take part in the regular reshuffling of the deck chairs on the *Titanic* that occurs in a federal government thrown off course by neoconservative foreign policies and neoliberal economic policies, but to turn the ship of state in a new direction. That turn, which will eventually be supported by Democrats, Greens, Libertarians, independents and, yes, Republicans of good will, is in a homeward direction—back to the Constitution, to the system of checks and balances and to the most appealing of all American principles: that the rule of law applies to every citizen, "be he President or be he pauper."

The political party that recognizes and embodies this truth will not be long in opposition, for it will speak anew the eternal language of Thomas Jefferson, the first democrat and the first Democrat. It was Jefferson who said, not in recollection of the founding of the American experiment but in warning to those who would defend it, "An elective despotism was not the government we fought for, but one which should not only be founded on true free principles, but in which the powers of government should be so divided and balanced among general bodies of magistracy, as that no one could transcend their legal limits without being effectually checked and restrained by the others."

CHAPTER 4

RULE-OF-LAW REPUBLICANISM

Conservative Crusaders Against the Imperial Presidency

I do not believe that our people can tolerate the formation of a presidential precedent which would permit any occupant of the White House to exercise his untrammeled discretion to take over the industry, communications system or other forms of private enterprise in the name of "emergency."

Representative George Bender,
Republican of Ohio, 1952

The power of impeachment is the Constitution's paramount power of self-preservation.

Representative Robert McClory,
Republican of Illinois, 1974

The point of impeachment, when proposed by patriots as opposed to partisans, is to define the presidency as a position that is accountable to the Constitution and the Congress. So it stands to reason that the most substantial impeachment efforts may go nowhere in any official sense but still have the practical and desired impact of holding an out-of-control executive's feet to the

George Bender

"I do not believe that our people can tolerate the formation of a presidential precedent which would permit any occupant of the White House to exercise his untrammeled discretion."

fire and of signaling to future presidents that they can and will be checked and balanced by the Congress. Those who understand impeachment merely as a political tool may lust after the image of a despised commander in chief being unceremoniously hustled out of the Oval Office, much as offending members of the Royal Court were once dragged from the castle in leg irons. But those who understand impeachment as a tool for maintaining the institutions that will always be more consequential than individuals to the health and welfare of the American experiment recognize that it is the demand for accountability that must take precedence, and that if this demand happens to be met by a means other than a House vote and a Senate trial, then the nation still has been well and truly served.

History reminds us that Republicans have recognized this dynamic and utilized it to a fuller and more fruitful extent than Democrats over the years, and this is to their credit. The Republican Party, with its historic distrust of concentrated power, has a better track record than the Democratic Party of recognizing the necessity of challenging excessive executives, no matter what their party affiliation. It was a former Republican president, Theodore Roosevelt, who, in 1918, offered the classic rejection of the false patriotism that would equate the support for a particular president with support for the nation—even in a time of mortal combat. "To announce that there must be no criticism of the president, or that we are to stand by the president, right or wrong," declared the twenty-sixth president as World War I raged, "is not only unpatriotic and servile, but is morally treasonable to the American public."

Yet, in an age when rank partisanship has mixed with professionalized political spin to drown both major parties in the swill of historical ignorance, most contemporary Republicans are unaware of their party's rich history of support for presidential accountability. Why? Because the stories of some of the most significant impeachment efforts initiated by Republicans have been all but lost to history. These most consequential of crusades do not fit easily into the shorthand with which the majority of historians deal with the impeachment impulse. As a result, in those rare moments when impeachment enters the limelight, journalists and politicos rely on an incomplete history that offers scant perspective on the full power and influence that the threat of impeachment has carried through American history. Ask a reasonably well-informed American how many presidents have been the targets of formal articles of impeachment; they will in all likelihood tell you that, at most, the number is three: Andrew Johnson, Richard Nixon and Bill Clinton. And they will be wrong. Articles of impeachment have been filed against nine presidents, in order: John Tyler, Johnson, Grover Cleveland, Herbert Hoover, Harry Truman, Nixon, Ronald Reagan, George H. W. Bush, and Clinton. In seven of the nine cases, Republicans—or, in Tyler's case, the Whig Party that would give way to the Republicans in the 1850s—were either the chief sponsors or major supporters of the impeachment initiatives. Indeed, it was the pre-Republican Whig Party that launched the first serious impeachment move against a president.

It is true that only two presidents have been impeached by the House of Representatives: Johnson, who assumed the presidency upon Lincoln's death and was targeted for removal by congressional Republicans in 1868, and Clinton, a Democrat who was the target of a Republican-led impeachment in 1998. It is equally well known that the full House would have voted for Nixon's impeachment, had the president not averted the crisis by resigning. But it is all but forgotten that the first full House vote on the impeachment of a president came in 1843, when Tyler, a Democrat turned Whig who had inherited the presidency after the death of President William Henry Harrison, was charged by Congressional Whigs with abusing his veto powers. Tyler avoided impeachment after the House split 127–83 on the issue, but he became known as "the president without a party," and the politically disemboweled executive would not seek reelection to a full term in 1844.

Of the five additional instances when articles of impeachment were submitted by members of the House, several provoked procedural votes by the full House, including two decisions—in 1932 and 1933—to table motions by Pennsylvania representative Louis McFadden, a renegade Republican, to impeach recently defeated president Herbert Hoover, a Republican who had just lost the election of 1932 to Democrat Franklin Roosevelt. McFadden sought to convince the Congress that Hoover should not be allowed to finish his term, arguing that as an example to future presidents the lame-duck executive should be sanctioned for misadministering the Federal Reserve Board, ordering troops to attack the unemployed veterans who had participated in the "Bonus March" on Washington to demand pension payments, and related "acts that stamp their perpetrator as one who is socially and morally unfit to be President."

But the "forgotten" articles of impeachment that surely mattered most in the development of modern American politics and, more precisely, in the vital work of checking and balancing the excesses of the executive branch never came to a House vote. They were submitted by a Republican member of the House whose name rarely appears in the annals of his party or his country, but whose service to the American experiment was of far greater consequence than that of most of his better-remembered contemporaries and virtually all the members of Congress who have followed him.

George Harrison Bender was one of the most conservative Republicans ever to serve in the House of Representatives, a fierce and unrelenting battler against Franklin Roosevelt's New Deal and Harry Truman's Fair Deal who stood for the House unsuccessfully in 1930, 1932, 1934, and 1936 before finally winning a seat representing the Cleveland area in 1938, which he held for

a decade and then lost in the 1948 election that saw Truman van-
quish Republican Thomas Dewey. Undaunted by defeat, Bender
was back in the House by 1951, reclaiming his seat for the last
two years of Truman's term. The Democratic president and the
Republican congressman would soon find themselves at odds in
one of the greatest clashes over the authority and power of the
executive branch America has ever seen.

In 1950, North Korean forces launched an assault on South
Korea that sought to secure the whole of the Korean peninsula
under Communist control. Truman—who had faced heavy criticism for failing to prevent a Communist takeover of China and
who feared that the anti-Communist "red scare" stirred up by
Republican U.S. senator Joe McCarthy and Republican U.S. representative Richard Nixon would paint Democrats as weak on
national security issues—decided that the United States would
join the fight over this distant parcel of land. Without formally
consulting Congress, he ordered General Douglas MacArthur,
who was in command of U.S. forces in Asia, to provide aid to the
South Koreans. He then chose to bypass Congress—disregarding
constitutional provisions requiring that a declaration of war be
approved by the House and Senate—and went instead to the
United Nations seeking justification for a dramatic commitment
of U.S. forces. Capitalizing on the temporary absence of the So-
viet Union's ambassador, who was boycotting the Security
Council to protest the exclusion of the People's Republic of
China, Truman secured approval of UN support for the South
Koreans. Because the United States was a member of the United
Nations, Truman argued that he had the authority to dispatch
tens of thousands of U.S. troops to the Korean peninsula and to
take action at home to support what was in everything but name
a war effort. So clearly was this fight identified with the presi-

dent, as opposed to the Congress, that it was broadly referred to as "Truman's war." "Truman and his supporters used semantics to defend the decision not to ask for a declaration of war," explained Donald Johnson, who served in the Forty-fifth Infantry Division during the Korean conflict, in a article written for the September 2000 edition of the *American Legion Magazine.* "If the word 'war' was not employed, the Truman administration tacitly argued, a president could send troops anywhere in the world for any purpose. Korea would be a 'police action,' the first of many such undeclared wars. And the constitutional system would be irrevocably altered."

In those early years of the Cold War, the Korea intervention was initially popular with the American people. Objections came from only a handful of members of Congress, most notably Senator Robert Taft, the Ohio conservative whose conservative supporters referred to him as "Mr. Republican." Taft had long expressed concerns about the penchant of presidents for making war without the full and steady approval of Congress, and the implications of such war-making at home. To allow a president a free hand, the senator argued in Madisonian terms, was not merely "contrary to the law and to the Constitution"; it would make the commander in chief "a complete dictator over the lives and property of all our citizens." An Old Right conservative who worried about spreading U.S. forces too thin in military adventures abroad, Taft echoed the founders when he warned against embarking upon international "crusades" that would have the United States "cover the world like a knight errant, protecting its friends and its ideals of good faith." "Nothing can destroy this country," he argued, "except the over-extension of our resources."

"So far as I can see," Taft said of the decision to commit U.S.

troops to the Korean fight, "I would say that there is no authority to use armed forces in support of the United Nations in the absence of some previous action by Congress dealing with the subject and outlining the general circumstances and the amount of the forces that can be used." As such, the Ohioan said, Truman's decision to commit ground troops to the Korean peninsula was "an absolute usurpation of authority by the President." Taft was, of course, right. As constitutional scholars Francis D. Wormuth and Edwin B. Firmage explained in their book, *To Chain the Dog of War: The War Power of Congress in History and Law,* "The Constitution is not ambiguous . . . The early presidents, and indeed everyone in the country until the year 1950, denied that the president possessed [the power to make war without congressional approval]. There is no sustained body of usage to support such a claim." But in that Cold War moment, Taft was fighting a losing battle not only in the broader sphere of national politics but within his own party. It was only after the experience of the Vietnam War, note historians of the right, that conservative thinkers such as Russell Kirk would come to celebrate Taft's vision, which newspaper columnist Nicholas von Hoffman would sum up well as a search for "a way to defend the country without destroying it, a way to be part of the world without running it."

One Republican who did agree with Taft, passionately, was his fellow Ohioan George Bender. Indeed, Murray Rothbard, the economist who was one of the last stalwarts of the Old Right conservatism of Taft and his followers, suggested that Bender often stuck closer to Taft's ideals than did "Mr. Republican." Bender was an outspoken conservative critic of Truman's engagement in what Old Right conservatives saw as "a reaffirmation of the nineteenth century belief in power politics" that guided the

United States toward a "policy of interventionism" that would fail to establish liberty abroad while undermining it at home. Bender's ideological comrade in the House, Nebraska Republican Howard Buffett—the father of Warren—summed up the view of the Taft men when he argued, "Even if it were desirable, America is not strong enough to police the world by military force. If that attempt is made, the blessings of liberty will be replaced by tyranny and coercion at home. Our Christian ideals cannot be exported to other lands by dollars and guns. Persuasion and example are the methods taught by the Carpenter of Nazareth, and if we believe in Christianity we should try to advance our ideals by his methods. We cannot practice might and force abroad and retain freedom at home. We cannot talk world cooperation and practice power politics."

Bender and Buffett saw the realization of their Madisonian fears of a republic given over to perpetual war-making on April 8, 1952, when Truman appeared on national television at 10:30 p.m. to declare, "At midnight the Government will take over the steel plants." Asserting that an impending strike in the steel industry posed a threat to national security, the president claimed that he was acting "by virtue of the authority vested in me by the Constitution and the laws of the United States, and as President of the United States and commander in chief of the armed forces of the United States." He ordered Secretary of Commerce Charles Sawyer to take immediate charge of the nation's eighty-eight steel mills. The next morning, U.S. flags were flying above the mills, and Truman had, in the words of his sympathetic biographer, David McCullough, "brought on . . . a constitutional crisis."

The *Washington Post,* a newspaper that was frequently

friendly to Truman, addressed the circumstance in a fierce editorial of April 10, 1952, which declared: "Nothing in the Constitution can be reasonably interpreted as giving to the Commander in Chief all the power that may be necessary for building up our defenses or even for carrying on a war."

The crisis was exacerbated a week later when, during a presidential press conference, Truman was asked whether the same "inherent powers" as commander in chief that he said gave him the authority to seize steel mills might also allow him to seize newspapers and radio stations. "Under similar circumstances the President of the United States has to act for whatever is for the best of the country," Truman snapped. "That's the answer to your question." The *New York Times* followed up with White House aides and reported the next day that "the president refused to elaborate. But White House sources said the president's point was that he had power in an emergency, to take over 'any portion of the business community acting to jeopardize all the people.' "

For George Bender, this was too much. The Ohio congressman filed articles of impeachment against the president, telling the *New York Times,* "I do not believe that our people can tolerate the formation of a presidential precedent which would permit any occupant of the White House to exercise his untrammeled discretion to take over the industry, communications system or other forms of private enterprise in the name of 'emergency.' "

Bender's impeachment resolution drew national attention, as well as support from a number of publications, including the *Chicago Tribune.* It was discussed at great length on network radio and television news programs, as had been a previous proposal to impeach Truman following the president's dismissal of General MacArthur, the commander of U.S. forces in Korea, a year earlier for insubordination. Appearing on the old CBS radio show "Capitol Cloak Room" several weeks after the seizure of the steel mills, U.S. senator Everett McKinley Dirksen explained, "I [have received] lots of mail that suggest that probably the impeachment course ought to be followed." Dirksen, an Illinois Republican who would go on to lead his party's Senate caucus for a decade, added, "I think it is a matter of course that must be seriously considered. Because if there [are] grounds for it then Congress certainly should not shirk its duty any more than a grand jury should shirk its duty . . ."

The half-hour program, broadcast in prime time, featured an extended discussion of the prospects for impeachment, with Dirksen, a former member of the House, answering questions not only about whether Truman had committed high crimes and misdemeanors but about whether the president's critics had "the votes to pass an impeachment article." The senator rejected the notion that a discussion of impeachment might best be put off because elections that would decide the control of Congress and the presidency were only six months off. On the question of timing, Dirksen was adamant, arguing that it would be dereliction of duty for Congress to defer action on impeachment in hopes that an election might resolve the issues at hand. Yes, of course, an election result could end the crisis in time, but, he said, "I don't [accept] it for a moment as a ground for being reticent about impeachment if the circumstances and the facts warrant that course be taken."

As it happened, it was not an election but rather the intervention of the courts that closed the discussion of impeaching Truman. Even as congressional Republicans were strategizing about how to force the issue in a House that was narrowly con-

trolled by the Democrats, the Supreme Court entered the space
that had been opened by Bender and his Constitution-quoting
allies, with the justices declaring, "Although this case has proceeded no further than the preliminary injunction stage, it is ripe
for determination of the constitutional validity of the Executive
Order on the record presented." Truman had expected the high
court, which was made up largely of Democrats, four of whom
he had appointed, to make a political decision in support of
the seizures. But in a charged environment, where talk of a
"Constitutional crisis" was on the lips not just of conservative
Republicans but even some liberal Democrats, Truman had miscalculated. Only a few hours after Dirksen told his CBS inter-
viewers that Congress could not "shirk its duty," the court
granted certiorari and scheduled arguments for May 12. The administration submitted 175 pages of documents seeking to establish that the precedent for sweeping presidential powers in a time
of conflict had been established by past presidential excesses.
They were trumped by the oral argument of the attorney for the
steel companies, John W. Davis, the seventy-nine-year-old former
solicitor general under President Woodrow Wilson who had
been the Democratic nominee for president in 1924. Quoting
freely from the Constitution and its authors, Davis closed with a
ringing paraphrase of Thomas Jefferson: "In questions of power
let no more be said of confidence in man but bind him down
from mischief by the chains of the Constitution."

Less than a month later, in a decision penned by Justice Hugo
Black, the court declared, "The Executive Order was not authorized by the Constitution or laws of the United States; and it cannot stand.

"The order cannot properly be sustained as an exercise of the

President's military power as Commander in Chief of the Armed Forces. The Government attempts to do so by citing a number of cases upholding broad powers in military commanders engaged in day-to-day fighting in a theater of war. Such cases need not concern us here. Even though 'theater of war' be an expanding concept, we cannot with faithfulness to our constitutional system hold that the Commander in Chief of the Armed Forces has the ultimate power as such to take possession of private property in order to keep labor disputes from stopping production. This is a job for the Nation's lawmakers, not for its military authorities," wrote Justice Black, who added, "The Founders of this Nation entrusted the lawmaking power to the Congress alone in both good and bad times. It would do no good to recall the historical events, the fears of power and the hopes for freedom that lay behind their choice. Such a review would but confirm our holding that this seizure order cannot stand."

Justice Felix Frankfurter wrote a concurring opinion that echoed George Bender's objections to Truman's power grab with a clarity that reminded its readers that jurists are never fully disconnected from the political debate.

> The Founders of this Nation were not imbued with the modern cynicism that the only thing that history teaches is that it teaches nothing. They acted on the conviction that the experience of man sheds a good deal of light on his nature. It sheds a good deal of light not merely on the need for effective power, if a society is to be at once cohesive and civilized, but also on the need for limitations on the power of governors over the governed. To that end they rested the structure of our central government

on the system of checks and balances. For them the doctrine of separation of powers was not mere theory; it was a felt necessity. Not so long ago it was fashionable to find our system of checks and balances obstructive to effective government. It was easy to ridicule that system as outmoded—too easy. The experience through which the world has passed in our own day has made vivid the realization that the Framers of our Constitution were not inexperienced doctrinaires. These long-headed statesmen had no illusion that our people enjoyed biological or psychological or sociological immunities from the hazards of concentrated power.

Bender's push for impeachment ended with the release of the court's decision. The presidential power-grab had been checked and balanced by the court. The ensuing years of the Cold War they sought to avert would not be generous with Bender and the other Old Right Republicans who created the space for a court packed with Democratic appointees—including Truman's former attorney general, Justice Tom Clark, the father of a future attorney general and proponent of impeachment, Ramsey Clark—to pull the reins on an individual president and, at least for a time, to slow the accumulation of powers that would lead the ablest historian of the era, Arthur Schlesinger Jr., to begin referring to an "imperial presidency." When Robert Taft died in 1953, Ohio voters elected Bender to fill out his term. But Bender's 1956 reelection bid failed and he died five years later in relative obscurity. Howard Buffett, who lost a 1954 Republican primary for a Nebraska U.S. Senate seat, retired from electoral politics. Colonel Robert Rutherford McCormick, whose *Chicago Tribune* had backed Bender and Buf-

RULE-OF-LAW REPUBLICANISM

fett in their hearty challenges to Truman, died in 1955. That was
the same year that William F. Buckley Jr. and his circle started the
National Review, a publication that would abandon the anti-
interventionism, the libertarianism and the rigid regard for the
Constitution in general as well as the system of checks and balances in particular that had motivated the Old Right. As the witty
and erudite Buckley and his magazine defined first the conservative movement and then the Republican Party, Rothbard wrote
in his brilliant 1990 essay "The Life and Death of the Old Right"
that "[mainstream American conservatism's] ideological transfor-
mation—into a warmongering and vaguely theocratic movement—was achieved by the early 1960s. The Old Right was
dead . . ."

And yet, there lingered on the right wing of the Republican
Party honest conservatives who continued to place their duty to
defend and preserve the Constitution ahead of their loyalty to a
president who happened to share their party label. So it was that,
in 1974, when the House Judiciary Committee took up the matter of Richard Nixon's impeachment, the Republicans who
broke with their party's president were not merely moderates
such as Maine congressman William Cohen—who famously re-
marked, "When the Chief Executive of the country starts to investigate private citizens who criticize his policies or authorizes
subordinates to do such things, then I think the rattle of the
chains that would bind up our constitutional freedoms can be
heard and it is against this rattle that we should awake and say no."
Conservative Republicans heard the rattle as well. The one Republican who voted for all three articles of impeachment that
were approved by the Judiciary Committee was Maryland representative Lawrence Hogan, a stalwart conservative who had pre-

viously made his name in the House by sponsoring a resolution declaring it to be the "sense of Congress that no pardon, reprieve, or amnesty be given to deserters or draft evaders." How was it that a staunch defender of Nixon's war in Vietnam could at the same time sponsor a resolution "to create a select committee to conduct a study of the precedents and Rules of the House regarding impeachment and to recommend to the House within 60 days, rules of procedure and practice for the consideration of articles of impeachment by the House of Representatives." Hogan saw no inconsistency. Indeed, he framed his opposition in terms of a consistent regard for the rule of law. Recalling the sometimes violent anti–Vietnam War demonstrations on college campuses and outside draft board offices, the Maryland Republican said, "[Violent demonstrators] felt that because their cause was just . . . they were above the law. They had long hair and beards and dressed as nonconformists and desecrated the flag. Inside the White House at the same time, there was another group of men who wore well-tailored business suits, close-cropped hair, no beards and wore flag pins in their lapels . . . They believed that the Viet Nam War was justified . . . They felt that because their cause was just they, too, were above the law . . . Now, obviously, both of those groups of people were wrong. Both should be held accountable for the violations of the law."

Hogan was one of seven Republicans—the others were Cohen, New York's Hamilton Fish IV, Virginia's M. Caldwell Butler, Wisconsin's Harold Froehlich and Illinoisans Tom Railsback and Robert McClory—who voted for at least one of the articles of impeachment against Nixon. Though the Democrats who controlled the Judiciary Committee had the majority needed to approve all the articles on party-line votes, a big-elbowed partisan split might well have saved Nixon. The calculus was summed up by a *Time* magazine report published the week before the committee voted, which explained,

> Most political observers in Washington believe that the committee will vote against the President and that the House of Representatives—probably late in August— will follow the committee's recommendation and impeach him. The Democrats, of course, have majorities in both the committee and the full House (248–187). But the size and character of the Judiciary Committee vote is regarded as a crucial factor in deciding whether the case against the President will also succeed in the Senate, where a two-thirds majority is required to convict the President and remove him from office . . . House leaders of both parties have long recognized that by far the most critical votes on the Judiciary Committee are held by the 17 Republicans. Their votes will count heavily if and when the articles of impeachment reach the full House and a trial in the Senate. If the committee Republicans stand almost solidly against impeachment, a critical number of other GOP Congressmen and Senators may be persuaded or pressured to do the same later on, and the President would stand a good chance of surviving in office. On the other hand, if four, five or even more of the committee Republicans support impeachment, other Republicans will find it easier to vote against the President in the full House and the Senate.

As the committee approached what *Time* referred to as "The Republicans' Moment of Truth," the Nixon administration pulled out all the stops. If not for the battering he had taken from the "liberal media," Nixon told an interviewer, Watergate would have been a "blip" on the political radar—amounting to nothing more than what the president dismissed as "the broadest but thinnest scandal in America . . ." White House press secretary Ron Ziegler identified Judiciary Committee chair Peter Rodino, a decorated World War II veteran who had been elected to Congress from New Jersey on the coattails of Harry Truman's 1948 landslide, as a "radical" who had turned the committee into a "kangaroo court" that had "made a total shambles of what should have been a fair proceeding." Wavering committee members were "invited" to the office of House Minority Leader John Rhodes, R-Arizona, for tutorials on party loyalty.

Yet when the "six days of decision" came in late July 1974, the rule-of-law Republicans cast the votes that sealed Nixon's fate. They did so because, as Hamilton Fish explained it, "The evidence is clear." But they were, as well, motivated by an understanding of the duty of the Congress to maintain the basic infrastructure of the Republic by checking and balancing the excesses of an executive temporarily entrusted with the keys to the Oval Office. Fish, whose father, grandfather and great-grandfather had served in Congress before him, explained that it was the committee's responsibility "to preserve the institution [of the presidency] by testing the fitness of the current occupant of that office against the standard demanded by the Constitution."

Fish's sentiments were echoed by Illinois Republican Robert McClory, a conservative stalwart who had arrived in the House in 1963 along with his friend, Donald Rumsfeld, to represent neighboring districts in the Chicago suburbs. McClory was a party man of the first order. But he was, as well, a Constitution man. Infuriated by Nixon's defiance of congressional subpoenas, the Illinois Republican argued that the president's refusal to cooperate with the committee represented an assault on the Congress and the Constitution. To the view of this constitutional scholar who, like another Republican named Abraham Lincoln, was proud of the fact that he practiced law in Illinois before coming to Washington, Nixon's contempt of the subpoenas attached the power of impeachment that had been accorded by the founders solely to the House of Representatives. Presidents have neither the legal nor political right to stonewall the House when it is investigating the high crimes and misdemeanors of the executive branch, argued McClory, who detailed Nixon's refusal to cooperate with the committee and declared: "Now, if you ever saw an example of stonewalling, the prime example is right there."

Yes, he was, like Nixon, a Republican. But McClory was first and foremost a member of the People's House and a defender of the powers entrusted to it by the Constitutional Convention of 1787. As such, he declared that he would vote to hold his party's president to account because, for Congress, "The power of impeachment is the Constitution's paramount power of self-preservation."

McClory's understanding of the duty of members of the legislative branch to zealously defend its authority may seem arcane today, when few members of Congress think of themselves as legislators first and partisans second. But his fear of encroachments by the executive branch on the powers entrusted to the Congress by the founders earned him plaudits from his constituents, who reelected him by a wide margin in 1974, and from at least one of his Republican successors in the House. Illinois representative Mark Kirk, speaking of his "political tradition" on the House floor in February 2001, said, "Congressman McClory represented Lake County and really serves as a symbol of independence in service to the nation. Congressman McClory, conservative, loyal Republican, a staunch defender of President Nixon until the evidence became too strong. It was Congressman McClory's votes for two impeachment articles that set the standard for political independence and judgment and the rule of law in this House."

While it may be painful for most Democrats, and perhaps even a few Republicans, to admit the fact, rule-of-law Republicanism would surface again in the late 1990s, when the House impeached former president Bill Clinton. There is little reason to doubt that the substantial majority of House Republicans who voted for the articles of impeachment against Clinton did so in precisely the "purely political, vindictive, partisan exercise" that, early in 1998, former House Judiciary Committee chair Henry Hyde Jr. had warned would fail. But time and experience have lent credibility to the view that some of the most determined Clinton critics were interested in something more than effecting regime change by a means other than the ballot box. Consider the case of Bob Barr, then a Republican congressman from Georgia, who as a member of the House Judiciary Committee was among the earliest and most ardent advocates for Clinton's removal from office. In the fall of 1997, before anyone had heard the name "Monica Lewinsky," the former U.S. attorney introduced H. Res. 304, a resolution directing the House Judiciary Committee "to undertake an inquiry into whether grounds exist to impeach William Jefferson Clinton, the President of the United States."

For Barr, it was never about sex with interns. He had become enraged at a much earlier stage in the Clinton presidency, after it was revealed that White House staffers had obtained confidential files on Republican officials, apparently for political purposes. "When we started looking at 'Filegate,' it became very obvious to me that something was very, very wrong," he explained to the *Washington Post* early in 1998, at a time when then–house speaker Newt Gingrich was telling Republicans not to sign on to Barr's call for an investigation of the impeachment option. "Initially, primarily watching the way the people in the White House operate, it raised some very serious questions in my mind. They didn't seem to care at all what the law allowed them to do or prohibited them from doing."

As he encountered more and more evidence of what he saw as serious violations of campaign finance laws on the part of the president and his aides, including what to the former federal prosecutor looked like a conspiracy to raise illegal foreign money and to provide beneficial treatment to the countries of those who gave it, Barr dusted off his copy of a 1974 report prepared by House Judiciary Committee staffers—including a young Hillary Clinton—titled "Constitutional Grounds for Presidential Impeachment." To the congressman's view, the grounds were there well before anyone was discussing whether Bill Clinton lied about having sex with "that woman, Miss Lewinsky."

"What bothers me is abuse of power," Barr explained, and the man who had once prosecuted a Republican congressman for perjury was more than willing to pursue the issue of a Democratic president's abuses.

"Well, how do we deal with it?" he asked rhetorically in a February 1998 conversation with a reporter. "Do we leave it up to the prosecutors? I don't think so. The Constitution provides the mechanism." Quoting Alexander Hamilton's reference to impeachment as "a political tool for a political offense," Barr announced, "In our system of government, the only vehicle we have to remove somebody from office if they abuse their office is impeachment."

When Gingrich and other Republican leaders, under pressure from their party's conservative base, finally decided to try to impeach Clinton, they did so without the broad focus that Barr had counseled. And while Barr was a public face of the endeavor, the former prosecutor found himself arguing a case that would appeal in its most salacious moments to moralizing social conservatives in the House but that never connected on the more fundamental abuse-of-power issues. So it was that a House essentially divided along partisan lines voted 228–206 to impeach Clinton for lying under oath when he testified before Independent Counsel Ken Starr's grand jury about the details of his extramarital affair with Lewinsky, but rejected an article that would have impeached the president for exceeding and abusing the powers accorded the executive by the Constitution. The December 2000 House votes confirmed an impression that the Republicans were engaged in what New York Democrat Jerry Nadler referred to as "sexual McCarthyism," rather than a serious move against executive excess. And the Senate's easy rejection of the articles of impeachment—with a number of Republicans joining Democrats in voting "no"—sealed the issue. Most congressional Republicans quickly retired from the arena of constitutional discourse into which their bungled attempt to impeach Clinton had drawn them, but Barr remained in the fight.

Three years after the House impeachment vote of 1998,

when the era of wonderful nonsense of the latter Clinton years had given way to the more sober—if not more legislatively sound—post-9/11 moment, Congress considered the disingenuously titled "Uniting and Strengthening America by Providing Appropriate Tools Required to Intercept and Obstruct Terrorism [USA PATRIOT] Act of 2001." The measure, a compendium of police powers rejected previously because of their dubious constitutionality, was being rushed by the Bush administration and its allies through the House and Senate before most members had a chance to read it. But Barr, who recognized the danger of permanently affording a president and his minions the powers contained in the act, fought to add a "sunset" clause to the measure. Appearing with Democratic representative Maxine Waters, a California liberal who had been one of Clinton's loudest defenders during the impeachment fight, Barr denounced the PATRIOT Act and smiled as Waters observed, "I find myself agreeing with Mr. Barr, and that is very unusual." After he was redistricted out of his House seat in 2002, Barr established a group called Patriots to Restore Checks and Balances and made common cause with the American Civil Liberties Union in the fight to defend basic liberties from assaults by the Bush administration. When the Patriot Act came up for renewal in 2006, Barr announced, "In a time where the president has authorized federal investigators to wiretap U.S. citizens living in America without warrants, we now more than ever need checks and balances on the federal government that will protect the fundamental freedoms of all Americans, no matter which political party holds the White House."

Barr was not the only Republican who broke with Bush over issues of executive power.

One of the great untold stories of the 2004 presidential campaign was that of the loud dissents against President Bush heard in Republican circles.

If the United States had major media that covered politics, as opposed to the slurry of self-serving spin generated by the White House and the official campaigns of the Republican and Democratic national committees, one of the most fascinating, and significant, revelations of the 2004 election season would have been that of the abandonment of the Bush reelection campaign by many veteran Republicans. But that story, for the most part, went untold—and most Americans, be they Republicans or Democrats, remain unaware of the extent to which loyal Republicans had grown uncomfortable with Bush even before his reelection. Scant attention was paid to the revelation that one Republican member of the U.S. Senate, Rhode Island's Lincoln Chafee, refrained from voting for his party's president—despite the fact that Chafee offered a far more thoughtful critique of George W. Bush's presidency than "Zig-Zag" Zell Miller, the dissenting Democratic senator from Georgia, did when he condemned his party's nominee. Beyond the minimal attention to Chafee's rejection of his party's president, most media completely neglected the powerful, and often poignant, expressions of concern and condemnation uttered by prominent Republicans—some of them close friends of the Bush family—with regard to the Bush-Cheney administration's abandonment of traditional Republican and conservative values.

Former Republican members of the U.S. Senate and House; governors; ambassadors; and aides to GOP presidents Eisenhower, Nixon, Ford, Reagan and George Herbert Walker Bush explicitly endorsed the campaign of Democrat John Kerry. For many of these lifelong Republicans, those ballots cast for Kerry were their first ever Democratic votes.

Angered by the Bush administration's mismanagement of the war in Iraq, its secrecy and its assaults on civil liberties, the renegade partisans tended to echo the words of former Minnesota governor Elmer Andersen, who said, "Although I am a longtime Republican, it is time to make a statement, and it is this: Vote for Kerry-Edwards, I implore you, on November 2." Objecting to the administration's use of "blatantly false misrepresentations of the threat of weapons of mass destruction" prior to the U.S. invasion of Iraq, Andersen argued that "this imperialistic, stubborn adherence to wrongful policies and known untruths by the Cheney-Bush administration—and that's the accurate order— has simply become more than I can stand."

Many of the Republicans who abandoned Bush expressed sorrow at what the Bush-Cheney White House and its allies in Congress had done to their party: "The fact is that today's 'Republican' Party is one that I am totally unfamiliar with," wrote John Eisenhower, the son of former president Dwight Eisenhower. But the deeper motivation was summed up by former U.S. senator Marlow Cook, a Kentucky Republican with impeccable conservative credentials, who explained in an article written for the *Louisville Courier-Journal* newspaper, "I am not enamored with John Kerry, but I am frightened to death of George Bush. I fear a secret government. I abhor a government that refuses to supply the Congress with the requested information. I am against a government that refuses to tell the country with whom the leaders of our country sat down and determined our energy policy, and to prove how much they want to keep the secret, they took it all the way to the Supreme Court."

Cook recognized a duty on the part of Republicans to hold Bush to account, arguing, "For me, as a Republican, I feel that when my party gives me a dangerous leader who flouts the truth, takes the country into an undeclared war and then adds a war on terrorism to it without debate by the Congress, we have a duty to rid ourselves of those who are taking our country on a perilous ride in the wrong direction. If we are indeed the party of Lincoln (I paraphrase his words), a president who deems to have the right to declare war at will without the consent of the Congress is a president who far exceeds his power under our Constitution."

Former U.S. representative Pete McCloskey, R–California, the man who on June 6, 1973, became the first Republican congressman to call for Richard Nixon's impeachment—on obstruction of justice grounds—was more succinct in his assessment of Bush, Cheney and their aides. "Nixon," explained McCloskey, "was a prince compared to these guys."

A few months after Bush began his second term, McCloskey expanded on his argument in an article for the *Sacramento Bee* newspaper that began, "The eerie parallels between the Richard Nixon and George W. Bush administration continue. Once again the famous words of Lord Acton in 1887 come to mind: 'Power tends to corrupt, and absolute power corrupts absolutely.' "

Sketching the comparison, McCloskey wrote,

Both Nixon in 1972 and Bush in 2005 won re-election to a second term. Both had impressive agendas for domestic reform, but both were at war—Nixon in Vietnam, Bush in Iraq. Both faced what they felt was disloyal, if not treasonous, conduct by former federal employees. Marine veteran Daniel Ellsberg had given the then top secret Pentagon Papers to the *New York Times* in 1971, and the *Times* risked prosecution for publishing excerpts, among which was the damning statement by Assistant Secretary of Defense John McNaughton that 70 percent of the reason for fighting the war was to save American face. The Nixon White House was desperate to discredit Ellsberg to preserve dwindling public support for the war—to allow a "decent interval" to elapse before South Vietnam fell to the North, in Henry Kissinger's words.

Nixon's chief domestic adviser, John Ehrlichman, ordered the burglary of Ellsberg's California psychiatrist's office to obtain records that he thought might show Ellsberg to be mentally unstable.

One of President Bush's stated reasons for going to war with Iraq was that Iraq had sought to purchase bomb-making materials from Niger. In 2003 respected former U.S. Ambassador Joseph Wilson said it wasn't so. Then someone high on the White House staff, equally desperate to protect the president's election, sought to discredit Ambassador Wilson by suggesting to the press that Wilson's wife, Valerie Plame, was a CIA agent who had suggested that her husband be sent to Niger.

Both in 1971 and 2003, the actions of these zealous presidential aides had dire results.

To McCloskey's view, the dire results begged a question: "Can it be that that awesome power has once again corrupted the aides and spokesmen for another Republican president?"

Before the year was done, that Republican president would be revealed to have authorized a program of illegal warrantless wiretapping of the phones of Americans that was so disrespectful of the Constitution that it inspired Republican congressman Ron Paul of Texas, perhaps the truest Old Right conservative in

the current House, to suggest that Bush's actions raised fundamental "questions about the proper role of government in a free
society."

While the president's defenders suggested that he needed to
be permitted to cut legal corners in order to defend the country
in the aftermath of the September 11, 2001, attacks on the World
Trade Center and the Pentagon, Paul was having none of it.

"Of course most governments, including our own, cannot
resist the temptation to spy on their citizens when it suits government purposes. But America is supposed to be different," the
congressman explained.

> We have a mechanism called the Constitution that is sup-
> posed to place limits on the power of the federal govern-
> ment. Why does the Constitution have an enumerated
> powers clause, if the government can do things wildly be-
> yond those powers—such as establish a domestic spying
> program? Why have a 4th Amendment, if it does not pro-
> hibit government from eavesdropping on phone calls
> without telling anyone? We're told that September 11th
> changed everything, that new government powers like
> the Patriot Act are necessary to thwart terrorism. But
> these are not the most dangerous times in American his-
> tory, despite the self-flattery of our politicians and media.
> This is a nation that expelled the British, saw the White
> House burned to the ground in 1814, fought two world
> wars, and faced down the Soviet Union. September 11th
> does not justify ignoring the Constitution by creating
> broad new federal police powers. The rule of law is
> worthless if we ignore it whenever crises occur.

Paul did not go so far as to call for the impeachment and removal of his party's president at that point, but another Republican, one of President Ronald Reagan's top legal aides, argued that a discussion of impeachment was in order. "On its face, if President Bush is totally unapologetic and says I continue to maintain that as a war-time President I can do anything I want—'I don't need to consult any other branches'—that is an impeachable offense," argued Bruce Fein. "It's more dangerous than Clinton's lying under oath because it jeopardizes our democratic dispensation and civil liberties for the ages. It would set a precedent that . . . would lie around like a loaded gun, able to be used indefinitely for any future occupant."

In 1997, Fein had written the article on "the merchandizing of the White House" that had formed the basis for Bob Barr's initial arguments for impeaching Bill Clinton. Barr, himself, proved to be a consistent critic of executive excess, declaring early in 2006 that "the American people are going to have to say, 'Enough of this business of justifying everything as necessary for the war on terror.' Either the Constitution and the laws of this country mean something or they don't. It is truly frightening what is going on in this country . . . The President has dared the American people to do something about it. For the sake of the Constitution, I hope they will."

The American people who identify as Democrats answered the call, for reasons both noble and self-serving. But what of the American people who wear the Republican label? Will a significant number of them have the courage of their rule-of-law Republican forebears to declare, "Enough is enough"? In the first months of 2006, some did just that. Referencing core conservative principles, author Thomas E. Woods Jr., in a prescient article for the journal of Old Right thinking in the dark passage of the neocons, the *American Conservative,* wrote,

> The lesson that all too many conservatives seem to have drawn from the Clinton years is not that executive power needs to be better defined and controlled but that it needs to be exercised by a Republican. Likewise, one might think two terms of a George W. Bush presidency would teach the Left a thing or two about executive power, but for all their carping at the president, most liberals seem quite happy with the status quo as long as the president issues executive orders on behalf of fashionable causes. Then when another neoconservative takes office and uses that power as George W. Bush has, the Left will trot out its now familiar routine of shock and indignation. Some opposition.
>
> Both liberals and at least some conservatives must share the blame for contributing to an ideological climate of which the inevitable outcome is the unrestrained executive under which our Republic now groans. Ultimately, though, apportioning responsibility for this transformation of the presidency, in which its occupant can flagrantly and defiantly violate the law, is of much less urgency than addressing—and, one hopes, correcting—the present debacle.

Could it be that honest conservatives will rise from the stupor that is imposed by hegemonic control of government and reassert an Old Right faith, the faith of George Bender and Howard Buffett and their kind, in the wisdom of the founders?

And might they, in so doing, redefine their party as a more con-
sistently principled organization either than its present self or the
Democratic opposition? In a fall 2004 article urging conservatives to vote against Bush's reelection, Scott McConnell, a founding editor of the *American Conservative,* argued,

> If Kerry wins, this magazine will be in opposition from
> Inauguration Day forward. But the most important bat-
> tles will take place within the Republican Party and the
> conservative movement. A Bush defeat will ignite a huge
> soul-searching within the rank-and-file of Republican-
> dom: a quest to find out how and where the Bush presi-
> dency went wrong. And it is then that more traditional
> conservatives will have an audience to argue for a con-
> servatism informed by the lessons of history, based in
> prudence and a sense of continuity with the American
> past—and to make that case without a powerful White
> House pulling in the opposite direction.
>
> George W. Bush has come to embody a politics that
> is antithetical to almost any kind of thoughtful conser-
> vatism. His international policies have been based on the
> hopelessly naïve belief that foreign peoples are eager to
> be liberated by American armies—a notion more
> grounded in Leon Trotsky's concept of global revolution
> than any sort of conservative statecraft . . . This election
> is all about George W. Bush, and those issues are enough
> to render him unworthy of any conservative support.

If Bush—and presumably Dick Cheney—proved unworthy
of conservative support in an election contest with a Democrat

to whom conservatives would be in immediate opposition, then, it holds to reason, the urgent matters of leaking previously classified information for political purposes, ordering illegal eavesdropping and otherwise abusing the powers of the presidency—all of which have earned the legitimate criticism of rule-of-law Republicans—ought to inspire honest men and women of the right to recognize the need to hold to account the current president in the same manner as did George Bender when he sought to impeach Harry Truman. Indeed, if there are certain constants in the American experiment, then, surely, two of the steadiest touchstones of conservatism across the ages have been a consciousness of the threat posed to basic liberties by big government and a faith that the American people will not long tolerate the "untrammeled discretion" of an executive whose accumulation of power is as abusive as it is excessive.

The lingering hold of that faith on a good many grassroots conservatives was confirmed early in 2006 when, after Senator Russ Feingold proposed censuring the president for ordering illegal eavesdropping on phone conversations in the United States, the American Research Group asked registered voters whether they thought Bush should be sanctioned as Feingold had proposed. Though the initiative had been rejected by most Democrats and roundly condemned by the Republican National Committee as something akin to treason, the voters surveyed favored censuring Bush by a margin of 48 percent to 43 percent. Predictably, 70 percent of Democrats wanted to rebuke Bush for approving warrantless wiretapping. But what was interesting was that 29 percent of Republicans, almost one-third of the GOP partisans questioned, indicated that they also favored censure.

Even more remarkable were the answers to another question

posed by the polling group:"Do you favor or oppose the United States House of Representatives voting to impeach President George W. Bush?" Even without any articles of impeachment under consideration in Congress, and without any significant national media discussion of the project, 43 percent of the voters surveyed expressed support for taking the step. As with the censure question, the strongest support for so sanctioning Bush came from Democrats, 61 percent of whom favored impeachment. Independents were about evenly split. And what of Republicans? A respectable 18 percent of the GOP stalwarts who were surveyed said it was time to impeach Bush. That represented a higher level of pro-impeachment sentiment among Republicans than was evident a few months before Richard Nixon stepped down in 1974, and provided a small indication of the discomfort with Bush among honest conservatives.

Just as there are Democrats who put their country ahead of their party, so there are Republicans who are similarly patriotic. Of course, the challenge of doing so is greater when a party has more to lose politically. But experience reminds us that, in the long run, it is more politically dangerous to defend the indefensible than to acknowledge the crisis and to address it from a place of principle. So it was that Republicans who broke early and explicitly with Nixon in 1974 were reelected, often by wide margins, while those who defended him to the end tended to suffer the consequences of standing on the wrong side of history. In the Democratic landslide of that year, Republicans who had recognized the necessity of sanctioning Nixon, such as New York's Jacob Javits and Maryland's Charles Mathias, were reelected with ease in Democratic states where they should have been vulnerable, as was Arizona senator Barry Goldwater, the conservative icon who saw off a serious challenge after leading the Republican delegation to the White House that convinced Nixon he would need to step down in order to avoid impeachment.

There will always be partisans who suggest that a president who shares their political label must be accorded blind loyalty. But this argument makes a political party into nothing more than a cult of personality, just as it dilutes the commitment to ideological values that should define a party more than any individual. For so long as the Bush-Cheney administration's lawlessness goes unchallenged by Republicans, that lawlessness will define the party to a greater extent than its ideals—a fact painfully confirmed for congressional Republicans by the polls of late 2005 and early 2006 that regularly found a correlation between declining approval for the president and collapsing support for his partisan allies in Congress. A principled challenge to Bush by rule-of-law Republicans would divide the party for a time, just as the principled challenge to Richard Nixon by key Republicans in Congress did in 1974. But for conservatives who have come to recognize that the president is no friend to conservative values or ideals, such divisions need not be frightening. Indeed, they could create the opportunity to which Scott McConnell referred in his call for Bush's ouster in 2004, the opening where "traditional conservatives will have an audience to argue for a conservatism informed by the lessons of history, based in prudence and a sense of continuity with the American past."

An impeachment fight provides something else that rule-of-law Republicans and traditional conservatives ought to value even more dearly than a chance to compete for the heart and soul of their party, and that is a chance to defend their country against the excesses not just of this president but of those future presidents—Republicans and Democrats—who stand to inherit all the powers that George W. Bush and Richard B. Cheney have claimed for themselves.

Every president defines the office he holds—for himself and for his successors—in a process shaped by his own demands and the counterdemands of the Congress. The president will, invariably, seek to define the authority of his position upward—not because he is, necessarily, a meglomaniac, and certainly not because he or she worries about the integrity of the office. It is simply easier to govern with no strings attached.

If a political party presumes that its members will control the presidency permanently, then the steady increase of executive power may seem a very fine idea—as such a pattern would appear to assure continuity of policies and programs over time, no matter what the vagaries of the unwieldy houses of Congress. But if a party presumes that its hold on the White House may be transitory—as has been the pattern from the founding of the Republic—then it encourages the accumulation of executive power at its own peril. The satisfaction that comes with the knowledge that a George Bush and a Dick Cheney are able to act as they may choose is great, but the horror that will come with the recognition that a Hillary Clinton or a John Kerry will take full advantage of the powers assembled by their predecessors could well be greater.

It is the promise of a partisan shuffle of power that imposes the duty of policing the presidency of one's own party on even the most passionate partisans. As the wise Republican congressman Ron Paul reminds his compatriots, "Conservatives who support the Bush administration should remember that powers we give government today will not go away when future administrations take office."

Abraham Lincoln

*"No one man should have the power
of bringing this oppression [war] upon us."*

CHAPTER 5

WHEN ONCE A REPUBLIC IS CORRUPTED

Impeachment in a Time of War

Congress alone is constitutionally invested with the power of changing our condition from peace to war.

President Thomas Jefferson, 1805

The provision of the Constitution giving the war-making power to Congress, was dictated, as I understand it, by the following reasons. Kings had always been involving and impoverishing their people in wars, pretending generally, if not always, that the good of the people was the object. This, our Convention understood to be the most oppressive of all Kingly oppressions; and they resolved to so frame the Constitution that no one man should hold the power of bringing this oppression upon us.

Representative Abraham Lincoln,
1848

I have a choice. I can either stand by and lead my constituents to believe I do not care that the President apparently no longer believes he is bound by any law or code of decency. Or I can act.

Representative John Conyers, Jr.,
2006

It was by the sober sense of our citizens that we were safely and steadily conducted from monarchy to republicanism, and it is by the same agency alone we can be kept from falling back."

Vice President Thomas Jefferson,

1797

In a democratic republic, the ideal tool for the removal of a dangerous or disreputable president is the ballot box. In the short history of the American experiment, the mere threat of an appointment with the electorate has led offending presidents, from Andrew Johnson to Lyndon Johnson, to voluntarily exit the political stage. But it is no secret that fear of the ballot box on the part of powerful incumbent politicians—and public confidence in the power of the ballot box to impose accountability—has eroded in recent decades.

The electoral check and balance on Washington elites has been attacked at virtually every turn. The antidemocratic gerrymandering of U.S. House district lines has rendered elections uncompetitive in all but a handful of regions nationwide. The free flow of special-interest contributions into the reelection campaign coffers of those same incumbents has made the prospect of opposing them even in volatile times a daunting one for potential challengers—particularly for challengers who would counter corruptions of the process by demanding accountability or reasserting traditional checks and balances on the politically powerful servants of privilege. Even the free press conspires against competition by neglecting political drama in favor of sensational tales of petty crime, bad weather and celebrity scandal. On those rare occasions when elections are competitive, their results are called into question by an electoral system so thoroughly inconsistent in its practices and results that it offers no guarantee that all Americans can vote or that their votes will be counted—as the contested finishes of the 2000 presidential voting in Florida and the 2004 presidential voting in Ohio well illustrate.

The combination of factors undermining confidence in electoral politics as a solution to what ails the American body politic has contributed to the greatest corruption of all in a system where citizens are to be their own governors: a deepening disconnect between the electorate and the election. Declining levels of participation in local, state and national elections, even when the competitions are held at momentous points in history, remind us that a "vanishing electorate" counting in the tens of millions no longer believes that voting matters, or that elections are anything but rituals—more akin to the ambitious coronation exercises of old that were meant to "legitimize" pretender kings than to a genuine contest over the direction of the nation.

In the first months of 2006, at a time when only about one-quarter of Americans surveyed by the Gallup polling organization said their country was "headed in the right direction," tens of millions of those same Americans told pollsters that they rejected the notion that casting a ballot in the next election could cause a genuine course correction. It is certainly reasonable to argue about the specifics of this rejection, and even to suggest that those who disengage are wrong to give in to cynicism. But it would be absurd to deny the reality of the disenchantment of the American people with their democracy. Even when they are offered an opportunity to select a new president of the United States, the most powerful player not just on the national but also the international stage, it is difficult to get half of the citizens who are eligible to vote to actually go to the bother of doing so.

While enthusiasm for American electoral politics has declined to what the U.S. State Department would identify as a "crisis of confidence" in the democratic processes of a developing nation seeking foreign aid from Washington, it is not so with impeachment.

Impeachment may be feared and reviled by the powerful, just as it may be enthusiastically embraced and encouraged by the powerless. But the discussion of the process, when it moves beyond theory to reality, is rarely dismissed as inconsequential or insignificant. When a full-scale and credible impeachment fight is in play—be it one that would come to be broadly viewed as legitimate, such as the 1973–74 struggle to remove Richard Nixon from the presidency, or even one that most Americans would come to see as a dubious endeavor, such as the 1998–99 stuggle to remove Bill Clinton—the nation becomes more engaged and politically volatile when the question of whether to abruptly conclude the tenure of a president is put in play. The great mass of citizens may cheer the process on, as they did when a Democratic Congress stepped gingerly toward the impeachment of Nixon, or they may grumble with dismay, as they did when a Republican Congress stumbled into the quagmire that the Clinton impeachment would become. Yet few are neutral, and many develop sophisticated critiques based on a better understanding of the Constitution's requirements for the removal of the president than they have of its requirements for the election of one—at least insofar as those requirements involve the Electoral College. Consider that, in the early stages of the Clinton

impeachment process, an October 1998 CNN/*USA Today*/
Gallup poll found that, while citizens who were surveyed opposed removing the president by 63 percent to 31 percent, they
split almost evenly on the question of whether the Judiciary
Committee should go ahead with impeachment hearings—48
percent in favor, 49 percent opposed.

The fact that tens of millions of Americans who wanted
Clinton to remain in office were able to put aside their personal
preferences and support going ahead with a process that might
lead to his removal illustrates the extent to which citizens understand that entertaining articles of impeachment in an official
forum is not merely a credible enterprise but, at times, a necessary
step in the maintenance of the American endeavor. After the
Clinton impeachment fight was finished, Pulitzer prize–winning
writer and editor Michael Gartner rejected the notion—pushed
relentlessly by Clinton's defenders and often accepted by his sex-
obsessed critics—that the impeachment vote of the House and
the trial in the Senate amounted to little more than a political
version of celebrity gossip. "This was the greatest human, moral,
political, and constitutional drama in our country since the end
of the Civil War," Gartner argued in a May/June 1999 *Columbia
Journal Review* article that was one of the few thoughtful post-
scripts to only the second presidential impeachment trial in the
nation's history. "It threatened to bring down a government and,
perhaps more significantly, turn the country into a parliamentary
democracy. It will reverberate forever. This was not just a lurid
story like that of O.J. Simpson or JonBenet Ramsey. This was a
drama about democracy."

From the nation's founding to the present day, this has ever
been the truth, and the genius, of impeachment.

Impeachment is not the antithesis of democracy, as the defenders of an imperial presidency would have us believe. Rather, it is an essential tool by which citizens, even those who have lost faith in the power of their own ballots, can be reconnected with the political process. Instead of choosing between the "lesser of two evils," an impeachment fight offers Americans an opportunity to ponder the question of whether a president or vice president is sufficiently evil, dangerous or incompetent to merit removal from office prior to the completion of a term to which he has been elected.

The point of these observations is not to suggest impeachment as a replacement for the electoral process. There must be a deeper justification for the removal of an executive than the desire to upset an unappealing election result before the next regularly scheduled vote.

But no one who is serious about American democracy—and certainly no one who recognizes the desperate need for democratic renewal in a country where the one thing that a Republican president, a Republican Congress and the official Democratic opposition to both had in common in early 2006 were approval ratings that hovered in the low thirties—should lose sight of the fact that the impeachment process provides an all too rare opportunity for an increasingly depoliticized nation to debate issues in a context that is more immediate and vital than what so many have come to see as an overly ritualized and often inconsequential election season.

This is, of course, as it should be in the United States. The founders of the American experiment, who expressed deep fears about the corruption of elections and the elected, saw in impeachment not a challenge to democracy but a tool for its rejuvenation in those predictable periods when decay would set in. Looking out toward the future from the precipice upon which the republic was founded, no less a participant in that creation moment than Thomas Jefferson predicted with certainty that "our rulers will become corrupt, our people careless. A single zealot may commence persecutor, and better men be his victims."

Of all the facts of the country's formation, perhaps none is so significant as that the founders established in the Constitution a specific set of procedures for the removal of presidents but did not establish a specific set of procedures for their election.

The founders were comfortable assuming that democratic processes would develop for better or worse over time, as they indeed did. But the crafters of the Constitution did not leave to chance the question of how abusive executives might be removed. The threat of what our third president referred to as an "elected despotism" was so feared that multiple steps were taken to provide citizens and their elected representatives with the power to check it. As was his practice, Jefferson explained the need for the fettering of the executive with a question: "What country can preserve its liberties if its rulers are not warned from time to time that this people preserve the spirit of resistance?"

It fell to Jefferson's closest comrade and successor in the presidency, James Madison—the father of the Constitution, whose notes provide the record of the debate that led to the inclusion of strong impeachment provisions in that document—to describe the circumstance in which basic freedoms were most imperiled. Writing to Jefferson in 1798, Madison observed, "Perhaps it is a universal truth that the loss of liberty at home is to be charged to provisions against danger, real or pretended, from abroad." If that danger, real or pretended, was met with the response of war, he argued, the commander in chief would quickly become the embodiment of that universal truth.

"Of all the enemies of true liberty, war is, perhaps, the most to be dreaded, because it comprises and develops the germ of every other," Madison explained in the volume of "Political Observations," which he penned in the early days of the Republic.

> War is the parent of armies; from these proceed debts and taxes; and armies, and debts, and taxes are the known instruments for bringing the many under the domination of the few. In war, too, the discretionary power of the Executive is extended; its influence in dealing out offices, honors and emoluments is multiplied; and all the means of seducing the minds, are added to those of subduing the force, of the people. The same malignant aspect in republicanism may be traced in the inequality of fortunes, and the opportunities of fraud, growing out of a state of war, and in the degeneracy of manner and of morals, engendered in both. No nation can preserve its freedom in the midst of continual warfare.
>
> War is in fact the true nurse of executive aggrandizement. In war, a physical force is to be created; and it is the executive will, which is to direct it. In war, the public treasuries are to be unlocked; and it is the executive hand which is to dispense them. In war, the honors and emoluments of office are to be multiplied; and it is the executive patronage under which they are to be enjoyed; and it is the executive brow they are to encircle. The strongest passions and most dangerous weaknesses of the human breast; ambition, avarice, vanity, the honorable or venal

love of fame, are all in conspiracy against the desire and
duty of peace.

To "chain the dogs of war," Madison observed, the Constitution "has accordingly with studied care vested the question of
war to the Legislature." There was no question that this was the
desire of the Constitutional Convention of 1787, where James
Wilson, one of the essential framers, told the ratifying session,
"This system will not hurry us into war; it is calculated to guard
against it. It will not be in the power of a single man, or a single
body of men, to involve us in such distress, for the important
power of declaring war is vested in the legislature at large . . ."

In 1801, the Supreme Court would confirm Wilson's assessment of the intents of the founders, with Chief Justice John Marshall writing of "the whole powers of war, being by the
constitution of the United States vested in Congress." In 1805,
while serving in the role of that "single man" to whom Wilson
referred, President Thomas Jefferson affirmed the standard once
more. "Congress alone," the commander in chief avowed, "is
constitutionally invested with the power of changing our condition from peace to war."

Jefferson, Madison and their contemporaries did not hesitate
to suggest that in a time of war, Americans faced a higher duty to
hold their presidents to account than in a time of peace. Madison,
in the letter that accompanied the draft of the Constitution he
dispatched to Jefferson on October 24, 1787, reflected on the necessity of the document's mechanism for "an easy & effectual removal by impeachment" of presidents who abused the powers
accorded them by the convention.

To make real the regulation of the executive branch, Madison warned that citizens would need to be most alert to such abuses in times of real or perceived threats to national security. It was for that reason that Madison reminded Americans in his great rumination on the Constitution, "Letters of Helvidius," that "every just view that can be taken of this subject, admonishes the public of the necessity of a rigid adherence to the simple, the received, and the fundamental doctrine of the constitution, that the power to declare war, including the power of judging of the causes of war, is fully and exclusively vested in the legislature; that the executive has no right, in any case, to decide the question, whether there is or is not cause for declaring war . . ." Because "the executive is the department of power most distinguished by its propensity to war," he explained, it was essential that the Constitution make available tools to "disarm this propensity."

The history of presidential powers in wartime has often returned to the necessary, if sometimes sobering, question of when it is appropriate to sanction the commander in chief for exceeding his authority.

A young Abraham Lincoln answered it in 1847 when, as a newly elected Whig Party congressman from Illinois, he charged that President James K. Polk had manipulated the country into war with Mexico on the basis of false complaints of Mexican aggression against the United States. Polk's justification for his decision to send U.S. troops into Mexican territory without a declaration of war was "from beginning to end the sheerest deception," argued the lawyer from Springfield who had been elected to the House of Representatives in 1846 as a critic of extending slavery into new territories. Lincoln well recognized that President Polk was a Southern sympathizer who was not above resorting to expansionist tactics in order to achieve such extensions and, accordingly, the congressman denounced Polk's war as "immoral, pro-slavery, and a threat to . . . republican values."

But Lincoln was not satisfied merely to articulate an antiwar position. Recalling Jefferson's counsel with regard to the nation's founding that "conquest is not in our principles. It is inconsistent with our government," the young congressman knew that, in order to prevent Polk from embarking upon a career of empire that might extend the reach of the United States—and of the Southern "slave power"—deep into Latin America, Congress would need to hold the president to account.

Noting the vague excuses that Polk had offered for ordering tens of thousands of U.S. troops into bloody combat and then assigning them the arduous task of occupying a foreign land, Lincoln grumbled that the president would have "gone further with his proof if it had not been for the small matter that the truth would not permit him." To emphasize this point, Lincoln introduced his "spot resolutions," which demanded that Polk—who claimed that he had chosen the course of war only after "American blood had been shed on American soil"—identify the precise spot at which a drop of American blood had been shed. "Let him answer fully, fairly and candidly. Let him answer with facts and not with arguments," the congressman said of the president. "Let him attempt no evasion, no equivocation."

When Polk did not answer, Lincoln told the House that it was because the president was "deeply conscious of being in the wrong." To counter that wrong, Lincoln made common cause with former president John Quincy Adams, a congressman from Massachusetts who dismissed the war as a Southern expedition to obtain "bigger pens to cram with slaves," in seeking first a formal investigation of the president's prewar statements and actions—as well as his use of a secret fund to pursue the endeavor—and then to formally sanction Polk for his lies and manipulations. Damaged politically by questions regarding his honesty and the necessity of his Mexican escapade, as well as the general malaise in a nation that was stumbling toward civil war, Polk announced that he would not seek a second term in 1848. But Lincoln, Adams and the "Conscience Whigs" who made up the antiwar camp did not believe Polk should be allowed to finish his presidency without facing congressional censure for his misdeeds. When a joint resolution honoring the service of Major General Zachary Taylor—who would be elected to replace Polk—was introduced in 1848, it was written so as to praise Taylor for his service "in a war unnecessarily and unconstitutionally begun by the President of the United States." Both houses of Congress endorsed the measure's harsh language with regard to Polk and his war.

Lincoln, who risked his political career in order to undermine Polk's mission, would explain to his Boswell, law partner William Herndon, that in challenging the president in a time of war he had engaged in the essential work of the republic:

> Allow the President to invade a neighboring nation, whenever he shall deem it necessary to repel an invasion, and you allow him to do so, whenever he may choose to say he deems it necessary for such purpose—and you allow him to make war at pleasure. Study to see if you can fix any limit to his power in this respect, after you have given him so much as you propose. If, today, he should choose to say he thinks it necessary to invade Canada, to prevent the British from invading us, how could you stop him? You may say to him, "I see no prob-

ability of the British invading us" but he will say to you "be silent; I see it, if you don't. The provision of the Constitution giving the war-making power to Congress, was dictated, as I understand it, by the following reasons: Kings had always been involving and impoverishing their people in wars, pretending generally, if not always, that the good of the people was the object. This, our Convention understood to be the most oppressive of all Kingly oppressions; and they resolved to so frame the Constitution that no one man should hold the power of bringing this oppression upon us.

If one understands the American experiment as an extension of the revolution that founded it and a continual struggle to uphold the Constitution that established the break with Britain as something more than a physical one, Lincoln argued, then criticism of a misguided president, particularly in wartime, is not merely allowed but required. To fail in the responsibility out of loyalty to a particular politician or party, or out of misguided patriotism, Lincoln told Herndon, "destroys the whole matter, and places our President where kings have always stood."

Lincoln's sense of the responsibility of a member of the legislative branch to uphold its end of the checks and balances equation offers essential instruction for contemporary members of Congress who may require prodding to recognize their duty to guard against the circumstance where "one man should hold the power of bringing the oppression upon us." Historian Stanley Kutler, who has written thoughtfully of Lincoln's challenge to Polk, recalled in 2003—as supporters of President Bush shrieked about how inappropriate it was to criticize the commander in chief once fighting has commenced—that it was "hardly a new ploy for presidential behavior" to suggest that once troops are committed abroad "then we must have a moratorium on criticism."

To counter the cynical and potentially dangerous "chorus for unanimity," Kutler suggested that a recourse to Lincoln was instructive. "Lincoln can help us," argued the historian. "He realized that he had to distinguish between the role of the military and the policies of President Polk. The army had done its work admirably, Congressman Lincoln noted, but the president had 'bungled' his."

Lincoln is hardly the only essential educator in the ways of dissent during wartime. Even as the sixty-year-old patriot spoke of raising a unit to join the fight in World War I, former president Theodore Roosevelt defended war critics who had been targeted for censorship, arrest and deportation by the administration of President Woodrow Wilson. In remarks that consciously recalled Lincoln's challenge to another wartime president, Roosevelt explained:

> Our loyalty is due entirely to the United States. It is due to the President only and exactly to the degree in which he efficiently serves the United States. It is our duty to support him when he serves the United States well. It is our duty to oppose him when he serves it badly. This is true about Mr. Wilson now and it has been true about all our Presidents in the past. It is our duty at all times to tell the truth about the President and about every one else, save in the cases where to tell the truth at the moment would benefit the public enemy.

> The President is merely the most important among

a large number of public servants. He should be supported or opposed exactly to the degree which is warranted by his good conduct or bad conduct, his efficiency or inefficiency in rendering loyal, able, and disinterested service to the nation as a whole. Therefore it is absolutely necessary that there should be full liberty to tell the truth about his acts, and this means that it is exactly as necessary to blame him when he does wrong as to praise him when he does right. Any other attitude in an American citizen is both base and servile. To announce that there must be no criticism of the President, or that we are to stand by the President, right or wrong, is not only unpatriotic and servile, but is morally treasonable to the American public. Nothing but the truth should be spoken about him or any one else. But it is even more important to tell the truth, pleasant or unpleasant, about him than about any one else.

It is often argued by those who would make the Constitution a historical relic, as opposed to a living document, that Jefferson, Madison, Lincoln and even Roosevelt could not imagine the age in which we live—a time of weapons of mass destruction, terrorism and the confluence of transportation, communications and globalizing impulses that so reduces the distance between the tumult of the world and the relative tranquillity of the American landmass. But the American president who best understood the requirements of modern warfare and the challenges posed by new weapons and new motivations for using them, Dwight David Eisenhower, echoed the counsel of the constitutionalists who came before him.

At the close of his presidency, Eisenhower called for con-

straints upon executive warmaking and the military-industrial
complex that he feared would create a permanent lobby on behalf of the imperial ambitions of presidents, explaining, "The potential for the disastrous rise of misplaced power exists and will
persist. We must never let the weight of this combination endan-
ger our liberties or democratic processes. We should take nothing
for granted." The thirty-fourth president warned the American
people, in words that recalled the founders while recognizing the
new realities of querilla warfare and terrorism, "Only an alert and
knowledgeable citizenry can compel the proper meshing of the
huge industrial and military machinery of defense with our
peaceful methods and goals, so that security and liberty may pros-
per together."

During the Vietnam War, the debate over that proper meshing became a subject of supreme significance. And that debate ultimately played out in a manner that would renew the structural
"spirit of resistance to government" that Jefferson so cherished.
In the summer of 1973, when the Congress was beginning to get
serious about investigating the Watergate break-in and the cover-
up by the administration of its links to that criminal endeavor and
related political "dirty tricks," a headline on the front page of the
Washington Post announced, "Impeachment Move Offered." But
this first resolution calling for the impeachment of a president
who remained relatively popular, was not a response to the Watergate high crimes and misdemeanors that would ultimately
cripple and then collapse the thirty-seventh presidency. Rather, it
was a move by Representative Robert Drinan, a Jesuit Catholic
priest and law professor who had been elected to Congress from
Massachusetts as an antiwar insurgent in 1970, to sanction Nixon
for failing to respect the Jeffersonian precept that "Congress

alone is constitutionally invested with the power of changing our condition from peace to war."

It had recently been revealed that Nixon had secretly ordered a massive bombing campaign against the nation of Cambodia, which hugged the western border of Vietnam. While the U.S. entry into Vietnam had not been authorized by a congressional declaration of war, presidents Johnson and Nixon asserted that—despite the reality that the arguments for its passage had long since been discredited—H.J. Res 1145, the Gulf of Tonkin Resolution, provided constitutional cover for the continued U.S. involvement in that country. Drinan disagreed, but he recognized that there was a debate on the issue. To the view of the constitutional scholar, however, there could be no debate about the fact that Nixon's secret order of the massive bombing campaign against Cambodia—according to White House transcripts, the president announced to aides, "I want gunships in there. That means armed helicopters, DC-3s, anything else that will destroy personnel that can fly. I want it done!"—represented an absolute violation of the constitutional requirement that wars be authorized by Congress.

On July 31, 1973, after the *New York Times* reporter William Beecher revealed details of how the initial carpet-bombing campaign had gone on for more than a year and killed tens of thousands of Cambodians, Drinan introduced H. Res. 513—"A resolution impeaching Richard M. Nixon, President of the United States, of high crimes and misdemeanors"—which citied violation of Section 1, Article 8 of the Constitution, "The Congress shall have power to . . . declare war, grant letters of marque and reprisal, and make rules concerning captures on land and water," as the grounds for congressional action. An embarrassment to House Democratic leaders, who were trying to mute discussion of impeachment at a time when they feared that challenging Nixon too aggressively could boomerang on them politically, Drinan's resolution was quickly assigned to the House Judiciary Committee. Despite committee chair Peter Rodino admonition to CBS News on the night of its introduction that the question Drinan raised was a "serious matter," the impeachment resolution attracted no cosponsors and languished in the file cabinets of the busy committee.

Almost exactly a year after its introduction, however, when the wheel had turned to such an extent that Nixon had in fact been impeached by the Judiciary Committee on Watergate-related grounds, a version of Drinan's resolution was finally considered in the closing discussion of the appropriate basis for sanctioning the president. With support from the Congressional Black Caucus, Drinan pressed the committee to move an article of impeachment against Nixon for ordering the bombing of Cambodia without the permission of Congress. Democratic leaders in Congress opposed the move, arguing that while the American people were prepared to impeach the president for the petty crimes of Watergate, they were not ready to remove him for violating the constitutional constraint against presidential war-making. They were foolishly satisfied with their new War Powers Act, a flimsy construct that wise members of the House and Senate, like California congressman Ron Dellums, had opposed because it gave presidents another excuse for end runs around the Constitution.

Drinan was having none of it. To the suggestion that an article of impeachment sanctioning the president for ordering the illegal bombing of a land with which the United States had no legitimately established grievance would not "play in Peoria," the congressman from Massachusetts asked, "How can we impeach the President for concealing a burglary but not for concealing a massive bombing?"

Drinan received unexpected encouragement from New York Republican Henry Smith, one of the committee's more ardent allies of the president, who suggested that waging war without a declaration was the one offense for which he might consider Nixon impeachable. Tragically, the committee's chief Republican backer of impeachment on Watergate-related charges, Maine representative William Cohen, lobbied against Drinan's Cambodia article on the bizarre grounds that the Congress itself had failed to serve as a proper check and balance against the president's seizure of war powers. "While this usurpation may have taken place, I happen to believe the usurpation has come about not through the boldness of President Nixon but rather on the default and sloth of the Congress," said Cohen. In effect, Cohen was arguing that because Congress had allowed the Constitution to be violated, it was precluded from correcting the violation.

Bill Clinton's future secretary of defense may have echoed the sentiments of the leadership of both parties with regard to the reassertion of congressional authority over warmaking, but he did not convince Drinan or younger members of the committee who had been elected on platforms promising to get the United States out of southeast Asia and assuring that the country would never again follow a course of quagmire. Thirty-two-year-old New York Democrat Elizabeth Holtzman—a Harvard Law School grad whose 1972 defeat of the previous chairman of the Judiciary Committee, forty-nine-year veteran and frequent Nixon ally Emanuel Celler, had altered the committee dynamic in a manner that made it possible to open the impeachment debate—was among the most outspoken proponents of sanctioning Nixon for the bombing order. She described the secret warmaking as being "in derogation of this system of free government and the participation of Congress." To those who suggested, correctly, that the previous Democratic president, Lyndon Johnson, was just as guilty as Nixon of waging an undeclared war, thirty-seven-year-old Utah Democrat Wayne Owens, who had also been elected in 1972 on an antiwar platform, was incredulous at the claim that past wrongs made it impossible for Congress to reassert the system of checks and balances. "I am amazed," Owens thundered, "that the argument can surface that the sins of the impeachable offenses, if they are, of one president [Johnson] can justify the same sins of another president [Nixon]."

Perhaps the most passionate advocate for impeaching Nixon for waging an illegal war was the forty-five-year-old congressman from Detroit, John Coyers Jr., who was then a relatively new member of the committee but who adhered to a relatively old-fashioned reading of the Constitution. "The one power of Congress that might, in fact, be more important than the power [of impeachment] that brings us here is the power to declare war," explained Conyers. "The president unilaterally undertook major military actions against a sovereign nation . . . I think a word should be said about it."

Conyers acknowledged that there were broader questions of presidential abuses with regard to the continuing quagmire in Vietnam, but he made the case that the committee should not deny the House an opportunity to use its impeachment powers to reassert a proper balance between the legislative and executive branches with regard to the declaration and conduct of wars. "We cannot absolve the fact that the Congress has failed to declare officially the war [in Vietnam] that has haunted us for nearly ten years," the congressman explained. "But we can use this moment as a new beginning . . . where the Congress says from this moment on, from this day forward, we will reinstate that law Constitutionally asserted from the beginning that somehow during the course of previous [Democratic] administrations, I am frank to admit, has eroded and we find that that power is no longer ours and ours alone."

The Conyers argument did not prevail in 1974. Drinan's Cambodia article failed by a committee vote of 26–12.

But Conyers did not go away. The Detroit Democrat remained on the Judiciary Committee, building up seniority with the passage of the years that would see the departures of Holtzman and Owens to make failed Senate bids and the exit of Drinan after Pope John Paul II demanded in 1980 that priests withdraw from electoral politics. Time would change Conyers' station in the chamber to which he had devoted his adult life. No longer the brash young liberal of 1974, he was, by 2006, the second most senior member of the House of Representatives and the last remaining member of the Judiciary Committee who had voted on the articles of impeachment against Nixon. Yet, in the most fundamental sense, Conyers remained the dogged defender of the Constitution that he had been on that hot July day when a dozen determined members of the House sought to restore the system of checks and balances.

Faced with new evidence of presidential wrongdoing in a time of war that one of the most prominent of the Watergate witnesses before the Judiciary Committee, former White House counsel John Dean, would describe as "worse than Watergate," Conyers became the congressional point man for holding the administration of George W. Bush to account—and for restoring a proper balance of powers between the executive and legislative branches. While it was true that his arguments for doing so recalled those that had failed to turn the Judiciary Committee against Richard Nixon in 1974, Conyers also echoed the line that Thomas Jefferson and James Madison had employed two centuries earlier when they set out to protect a new nation from the ravages of executive excess. Conyers saw, amid the lies and the failures of the Bush presidency, an opportunity to begin anew the American experiment on the foundations established by the men who handed to their successors the sword of impeachment along with George Mason's wise counsel to swing it hard and without apology against the "many great and dangerous offenses" of those who would abuse their authority.

At the Constitutional Convention of 1787, Mason fought successfully to broaden the definition of impeachable offenses to assure that "attempts to subvert" the Constitution would be included. And, as Conyers observed in 1974 and again thirty years later, there is no subversion greater than the misappropriation—through lies, false constructs and secretive scheming—of the power to declare war that had been afforded only to Congress.

When George W. Bush and Dick Cheney intrigued to wage war against Iraq in 2002 and 2003, Conyers was their chief and often lonely congressional nemesis. To be sure, there were other courageous members of the House and Senate who raged, often in the most inspired terms, against the dying of the light that had been kindled by the founders who declared that "we fought not for conquest." Robert Byrd, the venerable solon from West Virginia, roared like a wounded prophet of old against a "paralyzed" Congress that was "sleepwalking through history" as a reckless administration prepared to march the United States into a "destabilizing and dangerous foreign policy debacle" from which it would "reap disastrous consequences for years to come." Byrd, who carried a copy of the Constitution in the pocket closest to his heart, cried out in anguish as it was shredded by an administration and a congressional majority bent on proving true Jefferson's warning that "[we] should look forward to a time, and that not a distant one, when corruption in this as in the country from which we derive our origin will have seized the heads of government and be spread by them through the body of the people; when they will purchase the voices of the people and make them pay the price."

At times, as the war approached, Byrd seemed to be channeling Jefferson. This was particularly so when he preached from the great pulpit of the American experiment on the eve of the conflict that such war making was at odds with all America had stood for.

I believe in this beautiful country. I have studied its roots and gloried in the wisdom of its magnificent Constitution. I have marveled at the wisdom of its founders and framers. Generation after generation of Americans has understood the lofty ideals that underlie our great Republic. I have been inspired by the story of their sacrifice and their strength. But, today I weep for my country. I have watched the events of recent months with a heavy, heavy heart. No more is the image of America one of strong, yet benevolent peacekeeper. The image of America has changed. Around the globe, our friends mistrust us, our word is disputed, our intentions are questioned. Instead of reasoning with those with whom we disagree, we demand obedience or threaten recrimination. In-

stead of isolating Saddam Hussein, we seem to have iso-
lated ourselves. We proclaim a new doctrine of preemp-
tion which is understood by few and feared by many. We
say that the United States has the right to turn its fire-
power on any corner of the globe which might be sus-
pect in the war on terrorism. We assert that right without
the sanction of any international body. As a result, the
world has become a much more dangerous place.

But John Conyers was not willing merely to weep. With a
brilliant young attorney, MacArthur Foundation "genius grant"
recipient John Bonifaz, the congressman prepared a federal law-
suit that challenged the authority of President Bush and Defense
Secretary Donald Rumsfeld to order an invasion of Iraq without
obtaining a congressional declaration of war. At a February 2003
press conference announcing the suit, Conyers quoted Article 1,
Section 8 of the Constitution—"Congress shall have power . . .
to declare war"—and then looked up at the cameras to say, "Get
it? Only Congress." Bonifaz, reflecting his roots in the hometown
of the Boston Tea Party, explained, "The president is not a king.
He does not have the power to wage war against another country
absent a declaration of war from Congress."

Unfortunately, as Bonifaz would note in an interview with
the editors of Buzzflash.com, a political website, after the publication of his book on the prewar fight, *Warrior King: The Case for
Impeaching George Bush,*

[The] courts stood on the sidelines and refused to stop
this President's illegal march into war. And the courts
used a barrier that should not have been placed in the
plaintiffs' way to prevent any kind of judicial interven-

tion. They argued that Congress and the President were not in conflict, and therefore, there was no ability for the judiciary to intervene. Only if Congress and the President, on a matter of war, refused or were in conflict, then the judiciary could intervene and deal with that conflict.

Of course, that means that Congress can collude with the President to violate the Constitution and have the President send the nation into an illegal war, and the courts would have no ability to act. In fact, the courts have a specific duty to act to protect and uphold the Constitution, even if the other two political branches are colluding together to violate it. So here is a story of all three democratic institutions failing us—the executive branch, the United States Congress, and the federal judiciary. And the book is really sounding an alarm for our future, for the Constitution, and for the nation. We now have a new preemptive war doctrine articulated by this Bush Administration and it, combined with what's happened with the Iraq war, will impact the future of our country. We now have a precedent that any future Administration can effectively tell us that whenever they see a threat that perhaps the rest of the country doesn't see, the rest of the Congress doesn't see, the President alone can make the decision to wage war. These are powers held only by monarchs and tyrants, and it cannot be allowed that these powers should be held by the president of a democratic nation.

As the Bush presidency progressed, a litany of arguments for impeaching members of the administration would arise. In fact, though Conyers quietly convened meetings with Bonifaz and others to explore impeachment-related matters, one of the first serious mentions by a House member of the "I-word" came in January 2004 at the Sundance Lodge on Route 30, just outside Clinton, Iowa, where supporters of Dick Gephardt's campaign for the Democratic presidential nomination were rallying. No, the controversy-averse Gephardt did not make it, which was one of the many reasons why the former House minority leader's candidacy stirred little excitement. As it happened, the candidate's plane could not land at the Clinton airport because of fog. So Representative Jerry Costello, a stalwart Democrat from neighboring Illinois, hightailed it over to address the crowd on Gephardt's behalf. A member of the audience asked Costello whether Vice President Cheney's integrity was going to be an issue in the 2004 campaign. The congressman ripped into the pitch. "Could you imagine what the Republicans would be doing to a Democratic president who was a CEO of a company that now has gotten billions of dollars' worth of contracts—no-bid contracts—without competition?" Costello growled. "There would be hearings day after day. And my prediction to you is that you will see in this session of Congress that begins on Tuesday, there will not only be hearings but I think there ought to be impeachment hearings."

Although he may have been overly optimistic with regard to the potential for serious examinations of the wrongdoing of a Republican vice president by a Republican-controlled Congress on the eve of a national election, Costello had good reason to focus on Cheney. The man often described as "the most powerful vice president in history" is, as well, the most impeachment-worthy vice president since Spiro Agnew, the crooked former governor of Maryland who Richard Nixon joked was his own "insurance" against impeachment—on the theory that, much as they might hate him, congressional Democrats would never remove Nixon if it meant the presidency would fall to Agnew, a rabid reactionary best known for ranting that the nation's liberal intellectuals made up an "effete corps of impudent snobs" with a "masochistic compulsion to destroy their country's strength." Agnew, who at one point had invited an impeachment inquiry into charges that he had accepted bribes and evaded taxes—apparently on the misguided theory that the congressional action would forestall a criminal indictment—finally resigned in 1973 after pleading no contest to avoid a federal trial on the tax charges. Agnew's quick exit came before the House Judiciary Committee could take up separate resolutions by Representative Pete McCloskey and Representative Edward Hutchinson, a Michigan Republican, directing it "to conduct a full and complete investigation of the charges of impeachable offenses alleged to have been committed by Spiro T. Agnew." (Notably, a young congressman from Mississippi, Trent Lott, cosponsored the Hutchinson resolution.)

Agnew's relatively petty criminality, which involved taking kickbacks from Maryland construction firms, paled in comparison to the many charges against George W. Bush's vice president. The scandal of Cheney's lingering connection to Halliburton, his former employer—from which he continued to receive $150,000 annually in deferred compensation while serving as vice president, despite the fact that he was legally required to divest himself of such conflicts of interest before taking office, and to which the Bush-Cheney administration awarded contracts worth more than $9 billion—was only the first among many vulnerabilities. His internal and external advocacy for brutalizing prisoners of the Bush administration's so-called war on terror had been so aggressive that a *Washington Post* editorial described him as "The Vice President for Torture." As retired U.S. Army colonel Larry Wilkerson, who served as former secretary of state Colin Powell's chief of staff, told CNN in a 2005 interview regarding alleged White House misdeeds, "There's no question in my mind where the philosophical guidance and the flexibility in order to do so originated—in the vice president of the United States' office." Nor was there much question in Wilkerson's mind that Cheney and his neoconservative aides and allies formed a secretive clique that advocated within the Bush administration for policies of dubious legality that had created dire consequences for the United States.

After leaving the administration around the time of Powell's exit, Wilkerson told a New America Foundation forum in October 2005, "[The] case that I saw for four-plus years was a case that I have never seen in my studies of aberrations, bastardizations, perturbations, changes to the national security decision-making process. What I saw was a cabal between the vice president of the United States, Richard Cheney, and the secretary of defense, Donald Rumsfeld, on critical issues that made decisions that the bureaucracy did not know were being made. And then when the bureaucracy was presented with the decision to carry them out, it was presented in a such a disjointed, incredible way that the bureaucracy often didn't know what it was doing as it moved to carry them out." In addition to his policy intrigues, Cheney had involved himself in schemes of an impeachable nature to discredit critics of the administration's Iraq policies.

After it was revealed in April 2006 that the vice president's former chief of staff, I. Lewis "Scooter" Libby, had testified before a federal grand jury that Cheney had—allegedly with authorization from President Bush—ordered the disclosure of highly classified information regarding Iraq intelligence in order to discredit legitimate criticism of the administration by former ambassador Joe Wilson, Representative Maurice Hinchey, a New York Democrat, urged Patrick J. Fitzgerald—the special prosecutor in the CIA leak case that arose after the identity of Wilson's wife, CIA agent Valerie Plame, was revealed to the media—to expand the investigation to examine "the heart" of the matter. This, Hinchey argued, was the question of whether members of the administration conspired to lie to Congress and the American people about the reasons for going to war with Iraq—in particular by peddling a discredited claim that the Iraqis were attempting to obtain uranium for a nuclear weapons program—and then abused their authority to attack those who exposed the lies:

> If what Scooter Libby said to the grand jury is true, then this latest development clearly reveals yet again that the CIA leak case goes much deeper than the disclosure of a CIA agent's identity to the press. The heart and motive of this case is about the deliberate attempt at the highest levels of this administration to discredit those who were publicly revealing that the White House lied about its uranium claims leading up to the war. The Bush Administration knew that Iraq had not sought uranium from Africa for a nuclear weapon, yet they went around telling the Congress, the country, and the world just the opposite. When Ambassador Joseph Wilson, Valerie Wilson's husband, publicly spoke out with proof that the admin-

istration was not telling the truth on uranium, the administration engaged in an orchestrated plot, which now reportedly includes President Bush and Vice President Cheney, to discredit Ambassador Wilson and dismiss any notion that they had lied about pre-war intelligence.

Because of Cheney's long and close association with Libby—which began in the 1980s and continued through the administrations of both President George Herbert Walker Bush and President George Walker Bush—the prospect that the vice president might be the first to fall in a serious investigation of the administration's motives and actions was never lost on Hinchey, who had repeatedly called for a full congressional inquiry into Cheney's actions. "While many of us in Congress had long suspected that Vice President Cheney played a central role in the leaking of Valerie Wilson's name to the press, [news reporting of Cheney's role in authorizing leaks] confirms that there is merit to that belief," Hinchey declared in February 2006. "The leaking of Valerie Wilson's identity as a covert CIA agent is a very serious crime that jeopardized national security and everyone who was involved must be held accountable and brought to justice. No one, including Vice President Cheney, should be shielded from prosecution."

Hinchey was unaware of the fact that the second article of impeachment authorized in 1974 by the House Judiciary Committee against Richard Nixon had sanctioned the president for abusing the powers of his office to attack critics of the administration. While Republican defenders of the president dismissed Hinchey's assertions as the "conspiracy theories" of a partisan Democrat, the New York congressman had gone no further in his speculation about the inner workings of the Bush-Cheney White House than had William Cohen, who emerged as one of Nixon's primary inquisitors during the Watergate investigation. The Maine Republican had argued that it was entirely appropriate, indeed necessary, for congressional investigators to make the reasonable inference that the highest officials in the land had conspired to do wrong. "Conspiracies are not born in the sunlight of direct observations," Cohen counseled the Judiciary Committee in 1974. "They are hatched in dark recesses, amid whispers and code words and verbal signals, and many times the footprints of guilt must be traced with a search light of probability, of common experience."

The light of probability surely pointed to Cheney as each new revelation from Libby drew a clearer picture of the vice president's intimate involvement in the scheme to discredit Joe Wilson. Indeed, the *Los Angeles Times* suggested in April 2006 that the best service Cheney could perform for the Bush administration might be to pull an Agnew and resign citing "a concern about the publicity surrounding the trial of his former chief of staff, I. Lewis 'Scooter' Libby." Ultimately, however, the *Times* was less concerned about the vice president's mounting legal troubles than about the need for the administration to make a clear break with the neoconservative policies imposed upon it by the vice president, Secretary of Defense Donald Rumsfeld and their circle. Jettisoning Cheney, the editorial suggested, would provide "an implicit repudiation of the excessively hawkish foreign policy with which the vice president, even more than Rumsfeld, has been associated."

Of course, Cheney, a veteran of the Nixon and Ford administrations with a long memory and an oft-stated determination to "restore" presidential powers and prerogatives he believed had been undermined during the nation's brief period of accountability in the 1970s, was not resigning. And neither was Bush. Both men had set a course for their administration that admitted no weakness, respected no challenge and sought through secrecy and spin to thwart checks and balances upon its authority. Theirs was an imperial presidency. And it was clear to John Conyers that it demanded a counter rooted in the ancient struggle to tame those who believed they ruled by divine right.

As with Cheney, the bill of particulars that might form the basis for articles of impeachment against President Bush had grown long by the time the administration reached the midpoint of its second term. Along with Cheney, Bush stood accused by Libby of authorizing leaks of classified information, and by Wilkerson and other veterans of the administration of, at the very least, presiding over the "aberrations, bastardizations, perturbations, and changes to the national security decision-making process" that had characterized the darkest moments of his presidency. Among the many presidential acts that might qualify as high crimes and misdemeanors cited by lawyers with the Center for Constitutional Rights and other groups advocating for impeachment of Bush were his refutation of the Geneva Conventions regarding the treatment of detainees; his authorization of the practice of "extraordinary rendition," the extra-judicial procedure that allows U.S. authorities to send prisoners in U.S. custody to countries that are known to practice torture as part of interrogations; his presumed role as commander in chief in authorizing or encouraging military commanders and soldiers under his command to utilize torture as a means of interrogation; his failure to promote an aggressive and thorough investigation of the torture of prisoners detained in Iraqi prisons; his failure to respond quickly or effectively to Hurricane Katrina; his associations with convicted influence peddlers such as "super-lobbyist" and Bush campaign "pioneer" Jack Abramoff; and various and sundry other abuses of his office and the powers associated with it.

Even the Republican chair of the Senate Judiciary Committee, Pennsylvania senator Arlen Specter, suggested early in 2006 that "impeachment is a remedy" if it is determined that the president broke the law when he authorized his warrantless domestic spying program—a view shared by a majority of Americans, according to polls conducted at the time. Specter's comment was echoed, a good deal more firmly, by the conservative business journal *Barron's*, which noted, "Willful disregard of a law is potentially an impeachable offense. It is at least as impeachable as having a sexual escapade under the Oval Office desk and lying about it later. The members of the House Judiciary Committee who staged the impeachment of President Clinton ought to be as outraged at this situation. They ought to investigate it, consider it carefully and report either a bill that would change the wiretap laws to suit the president or a bill of impeachment. It is important to be clear that an impeachment case, if it comes to that, would not be about wiretapping, or about a possible Constitutional right not to be wiretapped. It would be about the power of Congress to set wiretapping rules by law, and it is about the obligation of the president to follow the rules in the Acts that he and his predecessors signed into law."

John Conyers would be outspoken in his criticism of the administration's illegal eavesdropping program. But it was the usurpation by the Bush White House of another power of Congress that concerned the Judiciary Committee veteran even more.

The fundamental issue of the president's conniving to com-

mit the nation to the invasion and occupation of a foreign land
without properly consulting Congress, let alone obtaining the required declaration of war, continued to haunt Conyers—as it
surely would have the founders to whom he returned continually
for guidance. Even as President Bush's poll ratings dipped to
Nixon-in-Watergate lows, it was still true that jousting with the
commander in chief on questions of his own legitimacy remained that most "daunting task" to which J. William Fulbright,
the chair of the Senate Foreign Relations Committee during the
Vietnam era had referred when he first began to mount his historic challenge to the Johnson administration's policies of intervention and occupation, which he correctly described as being
"marred by a lack of candor and by misinformation." Like Fulbright, Conyers took to the task with a measure of humility, but
also with courage and an energy that served as a reminder of why
the founders invested so much of their faith in the independence
of the legislative branch.

  Conyers brought his legal training, and his long experience
as the ranking Democratic member of the Judiciary Committee's
Subcommittee on the Constitution, to the task of building a case
for the consideration of impeachment. In May 2005, when the
Times of London unearthed the Downing Street Memo, Conyers
recognized the smoking gun. Declaring that "these allegations
strike at the heart of our democracy and present the most trou-
bling constitutional questions," the congressman penned the first
of several letters to the White House that were eventually signed
by more than 130 of his colleagues—all Democrats, although
Iowa Republican Jim Leach, a key player on international relations matters, would later sign California representative Barbara
Lee's House Resolution of Inquiry regarding White House communications cited in the British documents.

A final version of the Conyers letter, delivered to the White House in June 2005, read:

Dear Mr. President:

We the undersigned write to you because of our concern regarding recent disclosures of a "Downing Street Memo" in the London *Times,* comprising the minutes of a meeting of Prime Minister Tony Blair and his top advisers. These minutes indicate that the United States and Great Britain agreed by the summer of 2002 to attack Iraq, well before the invasion and before you even sought Congressional authority to engage in military action, and that U.S. officials were deliberately manipulating intelligence to justify the war.

Among other things, the British government document quotes a high-ranking British official as stating that by July, 2002, "Bush had made up his mind to take military action." Yet, a month later, you stated you were still willing to "look at all options" and that there was "no timetable" for war. Secretary of Defense, Donald Rumsfeld, flatly stated that "[t]he president has made no such determination that we should go to war with Iraq."

In addition, the origins of the false contention that Iraq had weapons of mass destruction remains a serious and lingering question about the lead up to the war. There is an ongoing debate about whether this was the result of a "massive intelligence failure," in other words a mistake, or the result of intentional and deliberate manipulation of intelligence to justify the case for war. The memo appears to resolve that debate as well, quoting the head of British intelligence as indicating that in the

United States "the intelligence and facts were being fixed around the policy."

As a result of these concerns, we would ask that you respond to the following questions:

1) Do you or anyone in your administration dispute the accuracy of the leaked document?
2) Were arrangements being made, including the recruitment of allies, before you sought Congressional authorization to go to war? Did you or anyone in your Administration obtain Britain's commitment to invade prior to this time?
3) Was there an effort to create an ultimatum about weapons inspectors in order to help with the justification for the war as the minutes indicate?
4) At what point in time did you and Prime Minister Blair first agree it was necessary to invade Iraq?
5) Was there a coordinated effort with the U.S. intelligence community and/or British officials to "fix" the intelligence and facts around the policy as the leaked document states?

By the time of the letter's delivery, more than 540,000 Americans had signed petitions urging the White House to answer the questions, and Conyers had convened a Capitol hearing that drew thirty members of the House for a discussion with John Bonifaz, Ambassador Wilson and former CIA analyst Ray McGovern, among others, of the issues raised by the memo and related documents that had surfaced in the British press.

The White House did not respond.

Conyers did not back off.

As the top Democrat on the Judiciary Committee, he directed committee staffers to begin an examination of the administration's words and deeds prior to the invasion of Iraq. By December 2005, that investigation had produced a 273-page report, "The Constitution in Crisis: The Downing Street Minutes and Deception, Manipulation, Torture, Retribution, and Coverups in the Iraq War." When he released the document, Conyers explained,

> In sum, the report examines the Bush Administration's actions in taking us to war from A to Z. The report finds there is substantial evidence the President, the Vice-President and other high ranking members of the Bush Administration misled Congress and the American people regarding the decision to go to war in Iraq; misstated and manipulated intelligence information regarding the justification for such war; countenanced torture and cruel, inhuman and degrading treatment in Iraq; and permitted inappropriate retaliation against critics of their Administration. The Report concludes that a number of these actions amount to prima facie evidence (evidence sufficiently strong to presume the allegations are true) that federal criminal laws have been violated. Legal violations span from false statements to Congress to whistleblower laws. The Report also concludes that these charges clearly rise to the level of impeachable conduct.

The reference to impeachment was explained in the recommendations of the report, which suggested the following:

Based upon our investigation of the conduct of this Administration, we believe that Congress must investigate the exact extent of the abuses of power and who was responsible, discipline responsible officials, and enact reforms that could deter such abuses in the future. In fact, failure to act immediately could not only indicate a desire that such abuses continue but also constitute an abdication of Congress's responsibility to act as a check against the Executive Branch. Explained in greater detail below, we recommend that:

1. The House should establish a bipartisan select committee with subpoena authority to investigate the Bush Administration's abuses detailed in this Report and report to the Committee on the Judiciary on possible impeachable offenses. Also, the House and Senate intelligence committees should have thorough hearings and investigate the Administration's apparent manipulation of intelligence.

2. A resolution should be passed censuring the President and Vice President for abuses of power.

3. Ranking Member Conyers and other Members should consider referring the potential violations of federal criminal law detailed in this Report to the U.S. Department of Justice for investigation.

4. Congress should pass, and the President should sign into law, legislation to limit government secrecy, enhance oversight of the Executive

Branch, request notification and justification of presidential pardons of Administration officials, ban abusive treatment of detainees, ban the use of chemical weapons, and ban military propaganda efforts.

5. The House should amend its Rules to permit Ranking Members of Committees to schedule official Committee hearings and call witnesses to investigate Executive Branch misconduct.

Explaining the first of the recommendations, the committee staff concluded:

The House should establish a bipartisan select committee with subpoena authority to investigate the Bush Administration's abuses detailed in this Report and report to the Committee on the Judiciary on possible impeachable offenses. Also, the House and Senate intelligence committees should have thorough hearings and investigate the Administration's apparent manipulation of intelligence. The select committee should complete its investigation within six months and, upon completion, report to the Judiciary Committee on any offenses it finds that may be subject to impeachment. Such a committee is needed because of the severity of the abuses of power and of public trust that may have occurred.

The Ervin Commission in the 1970's was instrumental in investigating the Watergate abuses of the Nixon Administration and led to the impeachment hearings in the U.S. House Judiciary Committee. In the past, the House also has created select committees to investigate serious breaches of public trust, issues of national security, or other matters of national concern. These have included potentially-illegal or unethical conduct by Presidents, such as the Reagan Administration's sale of weapons to Iran in the 1980's and U.S. military activity in Southeast Asia during the 1970's.

In this instance, we recommend that the select committee be comprised of members of the Committee on the Judiciary, Committee on Armed Services, Committee on Government Reform, Permanent Select Committee on Intelligence, and Committee on International Relations. Furthermore, the select committee should consist of equal numbers of Democratic and Republican Members.

In order to ensure it is able to obtain the information necessary to investigate the Executive Branch, the select committee should have the authority via a subpoena power to obtain documents relevant to its investigation. These documents would include, but not be limited to those in the possession of the:

- White House;
- Department of Defense;
- Department of Justice;
- Department of State;
- Central Intelligence Agency;
- Defense Intelligence Agency;
- National Security Council; and
- the CIA leak grand jury

Upon completion of the select committee's investigation, it should prepare a final and comprehensive report of its findings and any recommendations it has for amendments to federal law for improved oversight of the Executive Branch. In addition, the select committee should report specifically to the Committee on the Judiciary on any impeachable offenses it may uncover.

Conyers moved immediately to implement the recommendations of the report.

As the ranking member of the opposition party on the committee charged above all others with upholding the Constitution, he proposed that the Congress explore how and when to employ all of the powers at its disposal to hold the president and vice president to account—up to and including the power to impeach the holders of the nation's most powerful positions and to remove them from office.

The first of three resolutions introduced by Conyers, H. Res. 635, asked that the Congress establish a select committee to investigate whether members of the administration made moves to invade Iraq before receiving congressional authorization, manipulated prewar intelligence, encouraged the use of torture in Iraq and elsewhere and used their positions to retaliate against critics of the war.

The select committee would be asked to make recommendations regarding grounds for possible impeachment of Bush and Cheney.

The second resolution, H. Res. 636, asked that the Congress censure the president "for failing to respond to requests for information concerning allegations that he and others in his Administration misled Congress and the American people regarding the decision to go to war in Iraq, misstated and manipulated intelligence information regarding the justification for the war, countenanced torture and cruel, inhuman, and degrading treatment of persons in Iraq, and permitted inappropriate retaliation against critics of his Administration, for failing to adequately account for specific misstatements he made regarding the war, and for failing to comply with Executive Order 12958." (Executive Order 12958, issued in 1995 by President Bill Clinton, was written to promote openness in government by prescribing a uniform system for classifying, safeguarding, and declassifying national security information.)

A third resolution, H. Res. 637, would censure Cheney for a similar set of complaints.

Bonifaz, the lawyer who had sought with Conyers to check and balance the administration's rush to war in the spring of 2003, stood with him once more in the winter of 2005 to reassert the most fundamental of American principles. This time, they were not alone in recognizing that the battle lines had been drawn in a struggle over the Constitution itself.

"The people of this country are waking up to the severity of the lies, crimes, and abuses of power committed by this president and his administration," explained Bonifaz, who earlier in the year had founded, with veteran activists Steve Cobble, Tim Carpenter, Bob Fertik and David Swanson, the After Downing Street coalition, an alliance of more than one hundred grassroots groups organized to detail Bush administration wrongdoing and to encourage a congressional response. "Now," the attorney argued, "is the time to return to the rule of law and to hold those who have defied the Constitution accountable for their actions."

Bonifaz was right. The time had surely come.

But it was unlikely that the effort to censure Bush and Cheney, let alone impeach them, would get far without significant organizing outside Washington. After all, the House was controlled by allies of the president who—with a few honorable exceptions—had displayed no inclination to hold their commander in chief to account. Indeed, only a handful of Democrats, such as Conyers, had taken seriously the constitutional issues raised by the administration's misdeeds.

Members of Congress in both parties needed to feel the heat of citizen outrage if the resolutions that Conyers proposed were going to get much traction in the Congress or the country at large.

To that end, grassroots groups such as Progressive Democrats of America promised, in the words of PDA director Tim Carpenter, to "mobilize and organize a broad base coalition that will demand action from Congress to investigate the lies of the Bush administration and their conduct related to the war in Iraq."

In the months that followed, first a handful and then dozens of members of the House signed on to H. Res. 635, often after meeting with constituents organized by PDA and other groups associated with After Downing Street's "Censure Bush" campaign. Many of those who stepped up expressed their challenge to the administration in constitutional terms. Barbara Lee, the California Democrat who had been the first and loneliest champion of placing reasonable limits on the administration's pursuit of its "war on terror," spoke for all of them when she rejected any assertion that dissent must be silenced in a time of war.

What separates us from terrorists is not simply that our principles are deeply offended by the idea of torture or the murdering of innocents, but that we are a nation of laws. Our principles are enshrined in our Constitution and a system of duly enacted laws, and in a government where all are accountable and no one is above the law. Our Constitution gives us a system of checks and balances and divided powers because our founders were bitterly familiar with dealing with an unaccountable executive and were determined that our nation should not have a king, nor any office like it. The president and his advisers have tried to make this a question of whether we will defend our nation. This is misleading. Democrats and Republicans alike are committed to vigorously defending our nation. The real question is whether we will just as fiercely defend those principles that define our nation and separate us from terrorists, namely our commitment to constitutional government and our respect for the rule of law.

Conyers cherished the renewal of the discourse regarding the Constitution's charge to Congress to check and balance the president, particularly in a time of war. And he welcomed the burgeoning support. But the veteran congressman was not naive about the challenges that lay ahead:

There is a school of thought among Washington political consultants that criticizing the President about Iraq will make Democrats appear to be weak on national security. There is a media establishment that marginalizes politicians for espousing beliefs held by the majority of Americans. The right wing noise machine in turn retaliates against the President's critics. Be that as it may, I just could not be silent any longer. The title of the report is exactly right: the Constitution IS in crisis. There are serious and well-substantiated allegations that the Executive Branch has usurped the sole power of the Congress to declare war by deceiving the Congress about the evidence for war. There are serious and well-substantiated allegations that the Executive Branch has deceived the American people to manufacture the people's consent for war.

Ultimately, Conyers placed his faith in the power of the people to withdraw that consent, and to hold the president and the vice president accountable for their deceits.

It was a Jeffersonian faith, echoing the author of the Declaration of Independence's recognition that "every government degenerates when trusted to the rulers of the people alone." It was because of the certainty of that degeneration that Jefferson had said, "I know no safe depository of the ultimate powers of the society but the people themselves; and if we think them not enlightened enough to exercise their control with a wholesome discretion, the remedy is not to take it from them, but to inform their discretion by education. This is the true corrective of abuses of constitutional power."

The bitter experience of confronting the abuses of King George III led the founders of the American experiment to write a Constitution that empowered the people's tribunes—convened as the House of Representatives—to hold presidents and vice presidents accountable for their actions. The founders knew that those members of Congress courageous enough to raise a call for impeachment would succeed only with the support of an enraged citizenry. It would never be easy. But they were confident that the citizens who had safely and steadily conducted an infant nation from monarchy to republicanism would prevent it from falling back. They knew they would not live to join the battles over the fate of the republic that were sure to come. So they left behind the tool that would be required to maintain the proper balance of powers that is essential to realizing the promise of these United States in times of peace and particularly in times of war.

The founders did not fear that the impeachment of a president or vice president would create a constitutional crisis. They knew that impeachment was the proper response to the real crisis, and the only weapon strong enough to prevent the ravages of wars and warrior kings.

They spoke often of the difficulties that would be encountered by those who sought to defend the rule of law, especially for those, like John Conyers, who would stand in opposition not merely to an individual executive but to the premise of an imperial presidency. There would be pressure to compromise, to maintain a wretched status quo in order to preserve stability, to avoid "weakening" a president in a time of war.

But in the defense of their Constitution, the founders counseled no half steps or small measures. "When once a republic is corrupted," Thomas Jefferson explained in a notation written more for our time than his, "there is no possibility of remedying any of the growing evils but by removing the corruption and restoring its lost principles; every other correction is either useless or a new evil."

WHAT THEN FROM NEWFANE?

An afterword and a beginning

*Our country is in danger, but not to be despaired of.
Our enemies are numerous and powerful; but we
have many friends, determining to be free, and
heaven and earth will aid the resolution. On you depend the fortunes of America. You are to decide the
important question, on which rests the happiness and
liberty of millions yet unborn. Act worthy of yourselves.*

Joseph Warren, Boston Massacre Oration, 1775

It was appropriate indeed that the first opportunity for American
voters to express their sentiments on the question of whether to
impeach members of the Bush administration for high crimes
and misdemeanors came at a New England town meeting in a
community chartered two years before the Declaration of Independence was drafted.

In a country founded on the principle that executives—be
they kings or presidents—must be accountable to citizens, the
work of impeachment is best begun by the people, who Thomas
Jefferson identified as "the only safe depositories" of the American endeavor.

At the founding of the republic, George Mason, the father of

Ellen Tenney and Julia DeWalt

"When we witness what we believe in our hearts and know in our minds to be lawless acts, committed against the people of this great country, we must stand up and speak out."

the Bill of Rights, told the Constitutional Convention of 1787: "No point is of more importance than that the right of impeachment should be continued. Shall any man be above Justice?"

Two hundred and nineteen years later, in the Vermont town of Newfane, Dan DeWalt, an elected member of the community's select board, answered the essential question as Mason intended. "We have an immoral government operating illegally," DeWalt explained when he proposed that the good people of

Newfane, when gathered for their annual town meeting on March 7, 2006, should be invited to vote on articles of impeachment against George W. Bush.

DeWalt, who restores antiques for a living, had put himself to the task of restoring the proper balance of powers as defined by Mason and his fellow authors of the Constitution.

The erstwhile select board member gathered the necessary signatures to qualify an impeachment measure for consideration by his neighbors, who would gather on a late winter night in the southeastern Vermont town's 174-year-old Union Hall to consider the right governance of their community—and, as it happened, their country.

On the long list of issues set for consideration by the annual meeting, DeWalt's Article 29 would draw national attention for the first time to the annual meeting in a town that had held such gatherings each March since 1774.

The article that DeWalt penned was as concise in its language as it was precise in its intent:

Whereas George W. Bush has:

1. Misled the nation about Iraq's weapons of mass destruction;
2. Misled the nation about ties between Iraq and Al Quaeda;
3. Used these falsehoods to lead our nation into war unsupported by international law;
4. Not told the truth about American policy with respect to the use of torture; and
5. Has directed the government to engage in domestic spying, in direct contravention of U.S. law.

Therefore, the voters of the town of Newfane ask that our representative to the U.S. House of Representatives file articles of impeachment to remove him from office.

The defenders of the current regime began even before the town meeting convened to ridicule DeWalt for his audacious proposal, just as the defenders of a previous regime had mocked the colonials who convened to oppose it. King George III dismissed the American colonies as a region where "knavery seems to be so much the striking feature of its inhabitants that it may not in the end be an evil that they will become aliens to this kingdom." The court jester of another wartime ruler named George, Fox News Channel personality Sean Hannity, invited DeWalt to appear on his cable television program. In what has become the contemporary equivalent of the public denunciations of old, Hannity then proceeded to berate the Vermonter as an "idiotic" traitor who was "undermining" the military missions of the empire.

DeWalt, calm and dignified in the face of the attacks, did not back down. "As a patriotic citizen of this country, I need to stand up for what the country stands for," declared the dissenter, who promised to continue "living up to the Constitution, and the rule of law."

DeWalt was not naive. He knew that mockery and condemnation had always been the portion served up to those patriots who dared address the corruptions of empire.

It was not easy to challenge a King George in 1776.

It was not easy to challenge a President George in 2006.

But even the most conservative of the founders, Gouverneur

Morris, had reminded the Constitutional Convention during the debate on impeachment that a president must always be conscious of his secondary role in the scheme of the new republic.

"This Magistrate is not the King," explained Morris. "The people are the King."

And so in Newfane, on a cool March evening in the winter of America's discontent, the people were king. They judged the high crimes and misdemeanors of George Bush with a seriousness little evidenced along the corridors of federal power, as citizens weighed the necessity of the president's prosecution by legislators charged by the founders with the task of checking and balancing the excesses of the executive branch of government.

Recent history had assembled a set of facts, concerns and resentments sufficient to assure that the vote in Newfane would not be close. With Dan DeWalt reminding his fellow citizens that "in the U.S. presently there are only a few places where citizens can act in this fashion and have a say in our nation," the town meeting endorsed impeachment by a resounding margin. The paper ballot vote was 121–29 for the resolution.

To almost everyone's surprise that night, Newfane did not stand alone.

Word of the town's revolt had spread during the weeks prior to Town Meeting Day, and from communities across the region came reports of similar impeachment resolutions being introduced and passed. By the end of the night, five Vermont towns—Brookfield, Dummerston, Marlboro, Putney and, of course, Newfane—had expressed their determination to hold the president to account. The region's daily newspaper, the 130-year-old *Brattleboro Reformer,* embraced the movement, editorializing, "This nation can't take another three years of failed policies, reckless wars and a pervasive culture of corruption and cronyism. Vermont has led the way in the past. We can do it again. We hope Tuesday marks the beginning of a nationwide debate over the continued legitimacy of the Bush presidency."

In the weeks after the March 7 votes, the nearby town of Rockingham endorsed impeachment, as did Brattleboro, the largest community in the region.

Brattleboro's town meeting passed the most detailed resolution. The articles, authored by town representative Dora Bouboulis, read:

WHEREAS, Jefferson's Manual section LIII, 602, states that impeachment may be set in motion by charges transmitted from the legislature of a state; and

WHEREAS, George W. Bush had intentionally misled the Congress and the public regarding the threat from Iraq in order to justify a war against Iraq, in violation of Title 18 United States Code, Section 1001 and intentionally conspired with others to defraud the United States in connection with the war against Iraq in violation of Title 18 United States Code, Section 1805; and

WHEREAS, George W. Bush has admitted to ordering the National Security Agency to conduct electronic surveillance of American civilians without seeking warrants from the Foreign Intelligence Surveillance Court of Review, duly constituted by Congress in 1978, in violation of Title 50 United States Code, Section 1805; and

WHEREAS, George W. Bush has conspired to commit the torture of prisoners in violation of the UN Torture Convention and the Geneva Conventions, which under Article VI of the Constitution are part of the "supreme law of the land"; and

WHEREAS, George W. Bush has acted to strip Americans of their constitutional rights by ordering indefinite detention of citizens, without access to legal counsel, without charge and without opportunity to appear before a civil judicial officer to challenge the detention, based solely on the discretionary designation by the President of a U.S. citizen as an enemy "combatant," all in subversion of the law; and

WHEREAS, in all of this George W. Bush has acted in a manner contrary to his trust as President, subversive of constitutional government to the great prejudice of the cause of law and justice, and to the manifest injury of the people of the State of Vermont and of the United States.

Be it resolved that George W. Bush, by such conduct, warrants impeachment and trial, and removal from office and disqualification to hold and enjoy any office of honor, trust or profit under the United States;

WHEREAS, it is the uniform practice of the U.S. House of Representatives to receive petitions or resolutions from primary assemblies of the people;

Be it resolved that George W. Bush and Richard Cheney, by such conduct, warrant impeachment and trial, and removal from office and disqualification to hold and enjoy any office of honor, trust or profit under the United States;

Be it resolved further by the Town of Brattleboro,

that our Senators and Representative in the United States Congress be, and they are hereby, requested to cause to be instituted in the Congress of the United States proper proceedings for the investigation of the activities of the President, to the end that he may be impeached and removed from such office.

Be it resolved further, that the Clerk of the Town of Brattleboro be, and is hereby instructed to certify to the Clerk of the House of Representatives, under the seal of the Town of Brattleboro, a copy of this resolution and its adoption by the Town of Brattleboro, and that this resolution be entered in the United States Congressional Journal. The copies shall be marked with the word "Petition" at the top of the document and contain the authorizing signature of the Town Clerk.

The reference to "Jefferson's Manual," or *A Manual of Parliamentary Practice,* a book of rules of procedure and parliamentary philosophy written by Vice President Thomas Jefferson in 1801 that is still used by the House as a supplement to its standing rules, added a twist to the initiative that Dan DeWalt began. While impeachments have traditionally begun with a resolution introduced by a member of the U.S. House of Representatives, Jefferson's Manual—reflecting the sentiments of the founders regarding the need to provide multiple avenues for holding officials to account—outlined a variety of routes by which the impeachment process could begin. Jefferson explained, "In the House there are various methods of setting an impeachment in motion: by charges made on the floor on the responsibility of a Member or Delegate; by charges preferred by a memorial, which is usually referred to a committee for examination; by a resolution dropped in the hopper by a Member and referred to a committee; by a message from the President; by charges transmitted from the legislature of a State or territory or from a grand jury; or from facts developed and reported by an investigating committee of the House."

The reference to state legislators captured the imagination of Vermont activists, led by a former U.S. Department of Justice trial lawyer, Jeff Taylor, who proposed what came to be known as "The Rutland Resolution." Adopted around the time of the town meeting votes by the Rutland County Democratic Committee in central Vermont, the resolution read:

> WHEREAS, Section 603 of the Manual of the Rules of the U.S. House of Representatives provides for impeachments to be initiated on a motion based on charges transmitted from a state legislature, and
>
> WHEREAS, George W. Bush has committed high crimes and misdemeanors as he has repeatedly and intentionally violated the United States Constitution and other laws of the United States, particularly the Foreign Intelligence Surveillance Act and the Torture Convention, which under Article VI of the Constitution is a treaty as part of the "supreme law of the land."
>
> WHEREAS, George W. Bush has acted to strip Americans of their constitutional rights by ordering indefinite detention of citizens, without access to legal counsel, without charge and without opportunity to appear before a civil judicial officer to challenge the detention, based solely on the discretionary designation by the

President of a U.S. citizen as an "enemy combatant," all in subversion of law, and

WHEREAS, George W. Bush has ordered and authorized the Attorney General to override judicial orders for the release of detainees under U.S. Citizenship and Immigration Services (formerly INS) jurisdiction, even though the judicial officer after full hearing has determined that a detainee is held wrongfully by the Government, and

WHEREAS, George W. Bush has ordered at least thirty times the National Security Agency to intercept and otherwise record international telephone and other signals and communications by American citizens without warrants from the Foreign Intelligence Surveillance Court of Review, duly constituted by Congress in 1978, and designated certain U.S. citizens as "enemy combatants," all in violation of constitutional guarantees of due process, and

WHEREAS George W. Bush has admitted that he willfully and repeatedly violated the Foreign Intelligence Surveillance Act and boasted that he would continue to do so, each violation constituting a felony, and

WHEREAS, George W. Bush has violated the United Nations Charter and other treaties prohibiting aggressive war by invading Iraq without just cause or provocation, and has misled the US Congress by deliberate or grossly, wantonly negligent falsehoods to obtain the Authorization for Use of Military Force Against Iraq resolution (Public Law 93-102-1)

NOW THEREFORE the Rutland County Democratic Committee submits that his actions and admissions constitute ample grounds for his impeachment, and that the General Assembly of the State of Vermont has good cause for submitting charges to the U.S. House of Representatives under Section 603 as grounds for George W. Bush's impeachment.

The County Committee further submits that Articles of Impeachment should charge that George W. Bush has violated his constitutional oath to execute faithfully the office of President and to the best of his ability to preserve, protect and defend the Constitution of the United States.

In all of this George W. Bush has acted in a manner contrary to his trust as President, subversive of constitutional government to the great prejudice of the cause of law and justice, and to the manifest injury of the people of the State of Vermont and of the United States.

WHEREFORE, George W. Bush, by such conduct, warrants impeachment and trial, removal from office, and disqualification to hold and enjoy any offices of honor, trust or profit under the United States.

Quickly endorsed by eight other Democratic parties around the state, the "impeachment from below" movement swept Vermont in the spring of 2006 and quickly drew interest beyond the state's border.

While most federal legislators were slow to embrace moves to censure or impeach President Bush and other members of the administration, it was a different story with legislators outside the Beltway.

Two months after Newfane and the other towns cast their votes for impeachment, 69 Vermont legislators signed a letter urging the state's congressional representatives to push for investigations of the Bush administration that would likely lead to the removal of the president and vice president. The letter, penned by State Representative Richard Marek, suggested that Bush's manipulations of intelligence prior to the launch of the Iraq war, his support of illegal domestic surveillance programs and related actions had created a circumstance where Congress needed to determine whether the time had come for "setting in motion the constitutional process for possible removal from office." Noting that Newfane and a half-dozen other Vermont communities had called for impeachment, as had the state Democratic Party, Marek explained to the *Rutland Herald* newspaper, "Vermonters from across the state have expressed concerns with the president's actions and have displayed that through resolutions, meetings and petitions. I thought it was important to put our voices down as supporting an investigation and possible censure and impeachment."

The letter, which was delivered to members of the state's congressional delegation—including Congressman Bernie Sanders, a cosponsor of John Conyers' resolution on the subject—recognized that the composition of the Congress would make the pursuit of impeachment difficult. "We realize the serious practical difficulties of initiating even an initial investigation of these issues at present, much less in actually moving forward should they be substantiated," the state officials concluded. "However," they added, "speaking as individual members of the Vermont House of Representatives and the State Senate, we ask that you take all possible steps which you believe can lead to the initiation of such an investigation and then promptly conduct all further proceedings which are warranted by its results. We believe that Vermonters, our nation and our constitutional principles deserve no less."

At the same time that the letter was sent, a dozen Vermont legislators—members of the state's Democratic and Progressive parties and the Vermont House's lone independent—signed on to a resolution sponsored by State Representative David Zuckerman, a Progressive Party legislator from Burlington, asking for the state legislature to follow the route outlined in Jefferson's Manual and formally call on the U.S. House to open impeachment hearings. Arguing that the legislative resolution would carry more weight than the letter authored by Marek, Zuckerman rejected criticism of his move from state Republican leaders—and some cautious Democrats—who suggested that it was a waste of time for state legislators to enter the impeachment debate. "[No] president is above the law," he explained. "[This] is about a president who thinks he's king. We threw that notion overboard more than 200 years ago."

Zuckerman's words were echoed by California assembly member Paul Koretz, who submitted amendments calling for the impeachment of President George W. Bush and Vice President Richard Cheney, and from Illinois State representative Karen Yarbrough, who introduced a similar resolution around the same time in her state's legislature. "This president has acted as an emperor, not as a leader of one the three branches of government," said Yarbrough, whose proposal quickly drew a dozen cosponsors from across the Midwestern state. "People always talk about our founders and what their intent was," Yarbrough said of Jefferson's Manual. "With this, Jefferson's intent was pretty clear. He wanted to make sure there were checks and balances, and that there was this trap door." Even as she spoke, Republicans in Washington were scrambling to seal the door, telling reporters that a resolution passed by a state legislature would be assigned to the House Judiciary Committee, where, presumably, it would disappear into the same files that once contained the impeachment resolutions proposed against presidents Reagan and George Herbert Walker Bush by Henry B. González, the renegade representative from Texas who clung to the Constitution when others abandoned it in the 1980s and 1990s.

But the power of the impeachment-from-below movement, both symbolic and practical, was not lost on Dan DeWalt. In a democracy, reasoned the Newfane select board member who got the process started in his tiny Vermont town, it should matter when the people in direct votes at town meetings and through their legislative representatives call for presidential accountability. Declaring that "thanks to Jefferson, *we* have the power to force this conversation," DeWalt began working with representatives of the towns in southeast Vermont to deliver their impeachment resolutions to the office of Speaker of the House Dennis Hastert.

Ellen Tenney, a bookstore owner from Rockingham who had introduced the impeachment resolution passed by that community's town meeting, stood with Dan's daughter, Julia DeWalt, and a group of supporters outside Hastert's office on May 1, 2006.

Tenney read a statement she had written explaining her decision to travel from Vermont clutching the resolutions. "As citizens of the United States of America, we are honor bound to uphold the laws of the land, to defend the Constitution of the United States," she began.

> When we witness what we believe in our hearts and know in our minds to be lawless acts, committed against the people of this great country, we must stand up and

speak out. We are here today to demand that our elected officials in the US House of Representatives, Independents, Democrats *and* Republicans, fulfill their oath to uphold the Constitution of the United States of America, by instituting in Congress proper proceedings for the investigation of the activities of George W. Bush and Richard Cheney. I am holding here the first three Resolutions to be presented to Speaker of the House Dennis Hastert. These three Resolutions represent the will of my fellow Vermonters as well as the will of millions of patriotic Americans across the country.

The night before, Tenney had visited the Jefferson Memorial, from which a statue of the third president warily eyes the White House. At the feet of the man who had warned Americans to be ever vigilant in their watch against an "elected despotism," she gently placed copies of the resolutions.

In "Song of Myself," the epic exploration of what it might mean to be an American citizen, poet Walt Whitman wrote: "I speak the pass-word primeval, I give the sign of democracy . . ." As the pages of the Vermont resolutions fluttered in the breeze beneath Jefferson's statue, surely, the sign of democracy was given—across the ages, and in the spirit intended.

"Who are you, indeed, who would talk or sing to America?" asked Whitman. "Have you consider'd the organic compact of the first day of the first year of Independence, sign'd by the Commissioners, ratified by The States, and read by Washington at the head of the army? Have you possess'd yourself of the Federal Constitution? Do you see who have left all feudal processes and poems behind them, and assumed the poems and processes of Democracy? . . . Can you hold your hand against all seductions, follies, whirls, fierce contentions? are you very strong? are you really of the whole people?"

Came the answer, "Yes." From Newfane and Brattleboro and the towns of the Green Mountain State? "Yes." From the flatlands of Illinois? "Yes." From far California? "Yes." From these United States? "Yes." Echoing the patriots of generations past and generations yet to come, possessed of the federal Constitution, assuming the processes of democracy and holding their own against the seductions, follies, whirls and fierce contentions, the people spoke the password primeval. They gave the sign of democracy. To a country founded in revolt against inherited power and the royal prerogative, they had restored the faith of the founders. No more would they submit to despotism, inherited or elected. They would rise, as their ancestors had, to the defense of the American experiment. They would turn to their fellow citizens, as had Joseph Warren, the New England revolutionary who in 1774 drafted the Suffolk Resolves, that first bold declaration that subjects owed no loyalty to rulers who violated their rights. And these, the patriots of an impeachment revolution that, while new in specific complaints, was old in principle, would declare in the words of Warren: "Our country is in danger, but not to be despaired of. Our enemies are numerous and powerful; but we have many friends, determining to be free, and heaven and earth will aid the resolution. On you depend the fortunes of America. You are to decide the important question, on which rests the happiness and liberty of millions yet unborn. Act worthy of yourselves."

A NOTE ON SOURCES

Most books on impeachment fall into one of two categories: hand-wringing histories of "constitutional crises" and wide-eyed calls to use whatever tool is available to take down the maniacal monarch of the moment. Rare are the texts that argue, as this one does, that impeachment is not the cause of any particular constitutional crisis but the appropriate, if underutilized, cure. The notion that impeachment is a healthy tonic for the body politic is better understood by citizens than congressmen, better recognized by activists than academics. Thus, the study of impeachment as a process to be embraced rather than feared is best undertaken in the thicket of rebel tracts, founding-father notes, appeals to reason and dissenting opinions that make up the people's history of the United States and the empire from which our ancestors extracted themselves in 1776.

Original source materials form the backbone of this book, particularly those collected in *The Debates in the Federal Convention of 1787 Which Framed the Constitution of the United States of America* by James Madison, which was edited by Gaillard Hunt and James Brown Scott and published originally by Oxford University Press in 1920 and reissued in 1999 by Lawbook Exchange (Clark, NJ). Another useful text, *Journal of the Federal Convention, Kept by James Madison,* which was edited by E.H. Scott and originally issued in 1898, was reissed by Lawbook Exchange in 2003. The Avalon Project of Yale Law School collects many of the essential notes and documents online at http://www.yale.edu/lawweb/avalon/avalon.htm

Jonathan Turley's article "Senate Trials and Factional Disputes: Impeachment as a Madisonian Device," 49 *Duke Law Journal* 1–146 (1999), is a great historical and intellectual resource. A collection edited by Bernard Bailyn, *The Debate on the Constitution: Federalist and Antifederalist Speeches, Articles and Letters During the Struggle over Ratification,* was issued in 1993 by Library of America and hailed by Bill Moyers as "the best resource I've seen for understanding the morning headlines in a long time." As usual, Moyers got it right. Collections of the writings of James Madison, Thomas Jefferson and Tom Paine by the same press also informed this book, as have the research and writings of the brilliant Eric Foner, who edited the Paine collection for Library of America. Along with Howard Zinn, Foner is a historian who has well recognized that the struggle to control the presidential prerogative is essential to the American story.

It is necessary to read with a bold and adventurous spirit from the founding documents and the best histories of that time in order to reconnect with the original intent of the founders, which was to constrain the presidency. This understanding explains why they were so engaged with the process of defining the impeachment option, and why those who would seek to maintain the American experiment ought to share that engagement. Historian Ray Raphael's *Founding Myths* (The New Press, 2004) is important reading for those who seek to understand the beginnings of the American experiment, as is author Gore Vidal's essay "Homage to Daniel Shays." Additionally, Willard Sterne Randall's biographies of Jefferson and Hamilton, published respectively by Harper Perennial, an HarperCollins, are terrific resources. So, too is Garry Wills' 2002 biography of Madison for the American Presidents series published by Times Books.

The articles and texts mentioned above are referenced throughout this book. What follows are source references for specific chapters.

Introduction: Homage To Henry B. González

The world awaits the necessary biography of Henry B. González. The congressman's papers are housed at the University of Texas Center for

American History, and they are a true treasure for students of Congress and the Constitution. A fine review of the congressman's career, "The Legacy of Henry B. González," by Michael King, appeared in the *Austin Chronicle* on December 12, 2002, and provided useful insights and reflections, as did Jan Jarboe Russell's columns "Henry B. González" (January 2001) and "The Last Maverick" (July 2003) for *Texas Monthly*. An article by the congressman, "The Relinquishment of Co-Equality by Congress" (*Harvard Journal on Legislation* 29 [Summer 1992]: pp. 331–56), is essential reading, as are his comments contained in the Congressional Record, January 16, 1991, pp. H520–21. The Congressional Record also includes the other articles of impeachment mentioned in this chapter. Francis A. Boyle, the University of Illinois law professor who worked with González on the articles of impeachment against George Herbert Walker Bush, wrote a reflection on that initiative, which can be found on the FindLaw Legal Minds Community website at http://legalminds.lp.findlaw.com/list/forintlaw/msg00645.html. An Associated Press article published March 6, 1987, "Texan Acts for Impeachment," provides details of the response by González to the Iran-Contra scandal, while a March 29, 1989, article by David Johnson for the *New York Times,* "Meese Testifies That Impeachment Was a Worry," offers valuable perspective. A United Press International article published November 11, 1983, "Move for Impeachment Is Begun by 7 in House," reviews the move to impeach Reagan after the Grenada invasion. An article that provides perspective on concerns about high crimes and misdemeanors during the Reagan era, "Weigh Impeachment In An Illegal War," appeared in the *New York Times* on August 9, 1983; it was penned by former U.S. representative Don Edwards, who chaired the House Judiciary Committee's Subcommittee on Civil and Constitutional Rights at the time of its publication. *Lying Down with the Lions.* (Beacon Press, 1999) an autobiography by former representative Ron Dellums, written with his longtime aide H. Lee Halterman, provides excellent background on the fights over presidential authority that played out during the Nixon, Ford, Carter, Reagan, Bush I and Clinton years. This writer's review of that book appeared in *The Nation*, January 13, 2000. When I wrote an assessment of the careers of González and Dellums, which appeared in *The Progressive* magazine's February 1998 issue, George McGovern told me, "The real independents—the people who are willing to stand up to pressures of the moment on behalf of the future—are disappearing from Congress."

Representative Marcy Kaptur, Democrat of Ohio, one of the boldest members of the House, told me, "Too many people in Congress today are Lilliputians. They can't see the big picture. Those two men, Ron Dellums and Henry González, they saw the big picture and they dedicated their careers to lofty purposes. I shudder to think of a Congress without them."

Chapter 1: The Genius of Impeachment

Woody Allen's book *Four Films* (Random House) includes the *Annie Hall* script. The *Time* magazine cover story "The Push to Impeach" appeared November 5, 1973. *Time*'s coverage of the Watergate debate from around the country was generally excellent. It informs this chapter and is highly recommended reading, as is the coverage from *The Nation,* which I reviewed in preparation for this project. *Playboy*'s interview with Hunter Thompson appeared in the November 1974 issue. Garry Trudeau's Watergate-era *Doonesbury* cartoons appear in the book *Guilty, Guilty, Guilty!* (Henry Holt & Co, 1974).

Stanley Kutler's *The Wars of Watergate* (W. W. Norton & Company, 1992) remains the essential text for anyone seeking an in-depth assessment of the long struggle. The transcripts of the House Judiciary Committee's sessions can be found in "U.S. House of Representatives: House Committee on the Judiciary Impeachment of Richard M. Nixon, President of the United States, 93d Cong., 2d sess., 1974," H. Rept. 93-1305. The best source of information regarding the Iran-Contra scandal and the congressional response to it is *The Iran-Contra Affair: The Making of a Scandal, 1983–1988,* the collection of 4,635 documents totaling approximately 14,000 pages pulled together by the National Security Archive. You can visit it on the web at the Digital National Security Archive: http://nsarchive.chadwyck.com/icintro.htm.

In my book *The Rise and Rise of Richard B. Cheney* (The New Press: 2004), I wrote extensively about Dick Cheney's attitudes regarding presidential powers. Former White House counsel John Dean was a tremendously useful source for that book, and his FindLaw columns on Cheney are essential reading, as is his book *Worse Than Watergate* (Little, Brown, 2004). For Cheney's recent thinking regarding presidential powers, review "A Strong Executive," the *Wall Street Journal,* January 28, 2006. Robert Byrd delivered his speech "Protecting the Constitutional Authorities of Congress" to the Senate on April 11, 2003. A collection of his speeches about this and related issues, *Losing America* (W.W. Norton & Company), was published in 2004.

For an examination of concerns regarding the Clinton administration's abuse of war powers see "Where Are the Doves in Congress?" by John Nichols, *The Progressive* (October 1999). Feingold's comparison of the Nixon and Bush eras was delivered February 7, 2006, as part of a Senate floor statement on the Bush administration's warrantless wiretapping initiative. See also "Feingold Moves to Censure Bush" by John Nichols, *The Nation,* March 13, 2006. Elizabeth Holtzman's article "The Impeachment of George W. Bush" appeared in *The Nation,* January 30, 2006.

Chapter 2: A Live Instrument of the Constitution

The Burke quote that begins this chapter, along with other Burke quotes in the chapter, can be found in *The Works Of The Right Honourable Edmund Burke* (Little, Brown & Company, 1901).

The *Times* of London's reporting on the Downing Street Memo is found in a number of articles, the most useful of which is "Blair Planned Iraq War From the Start" by Michael Smith, May 1, 2005. The newspaper published portions of the documents it had obtained the same day under the headline "The Secret Downing Street Memo." Dan Plesch's article "There is Always Impeachment" appeared January 28, 2004, in the *Guardian*. Another important article by Plesch, "The Case for Impeachment," September 22, 2004, also appeared in the *Guardian*. His article "Why Blair Should Be Impeached" appeared November 28, 2004, in Scotland's *Sunday Herald,* and his article "Tony Blair. You Are Charged With Leading Britain Into an Illegal War . . . How Do You Plead?" appeared in the same newspaper on May 27, 2005. The book Plesch wrote with Glen Rangwala, *A Case to Answer,* was published by Spokesman Books in 2004. For more on the book and the movement to impeach Blair, visit http://www.impeachblair.net/. For the House of Commons Library monograph on impeachment, visit http://www.parliament.uk/commons/lib/research/notes/snpc-02666.pdf.

Adam Price's article "Now for the Politics of Last Resort: Impeach Tony Blair" appeared August 26, 2004, in the *Guardian*. Price's "101 Parliamentary Questions on Iraq for the Prime Minister" was tabled in Parliament on September 6, 2004. Boris Johnson's "Isn't it time to impeach Blair over Iraq?" appeared August 26, 2004, in the *Telegraph*. The *Spectator's* editorial on impeachment appeared August 28, 2004. A very good review of the impeachment drive by political writer Alison Hardie appeared August 26, 2004, in the *Scotsman* newspaper under the headline "MPs Launch Bid to Impeach Blair." The *Guardian's* article on the impeachment initiative "MPs Plan to Impeach Blair Over Iraq War Record," by Westminster correspondent David Hencke, appeared August 27, 2004. Hencke's article "Commons Motion to Impeach Blair Gets Go-Ahead" was published November 19, 2004.

BOPCRIS (British Official Publications Collaborative Reader Information Service) serves as a clearinghouse for official documents from British history and was an invaluable resource for this project. Matthew Romney's "The Origins and Scope of Presidential Impeachment" appeared in the University of Utah's *Hinckley Journal of Politics,* Spring 2000, Vol. 2, No. 1, pp. 67–72. Simon Schama's *A History of Britain* (Miramax Books, 2000) is a useful text for Americans trying to keep their King Richards straight. For specific details of Burke's involvement in the Hastings trial, see "India: The Hastings Trial, 1789–1794" in *The Writings and Speeches of Edmund Burke,* volume 7, edited by Peter J. Marshall (Clarendon Press, 2000). See also a very fine 1989 book, *The Impeachment of Warren Hastings* (Edinburgh University Press), edited by C. E. Nicholson and Geoffrey Carnell.

Buckner F. Melton Jr.'s *The First Impeachment* (Mercer University Press, 1998) provides useful background on impeachments in the colonial era and the early days of the United States. The American Civil Liberties Union pamphlet from 1973 *Impeachment: What You Can Do* provides a good short history, as does "The Law of Presidential Impeachment," a paper prepared in 1974 by the Association of the Bar of the City of New York, Committee on Federal Legislation. The November 9, 1998, testimony of Daniel H. Pollitt, the Kenan Professor of Law, Emeritus, University of North Carolina Law School, to the House Judiciary Committee Subcommittee on the Constitution covers many of the same points. Pollitt's testimony was delivered as part of a hearing on the background and history of impeachment that was part of the Clinton impeachment debate. Finally, the second edition of Michael Gerhardt's *The Federal Impeachment Process* (University of Chicago Press, 2000) is an excellent resource that informs any discussion of the development of impeachment as a tool for holding presidents to account.

For more on Peter Kilfoyle and the British impeachment campaign, see Plesch, "There is Always Impeachment," and Ewen MacAskill and Richard Norton-Taylor, "Fight to impeach Blair gains support: Campaigners confident of forcing debate in Commons," which appeared in the *Guardian* newspaper, September 17, 2004. The Keith Vaz critique can be found in "Blair Impeachment Campaign Starts," BBC News, August 27, 2004, and " 'Impeach Blair' Wins Legal Backing," BBC News, September 23, 2004. Garnier's comment on "the No 10 machinists" can be found in Isabel Hilton, "The Ditch Blair Project," *Financial Times,* March 4, 2005. For more on the Commons motion and support for it, see "Stars Back Attempt to Impeach Blair" by Andrew

Sparrow, the *Daily Telegraph,* November 25, 2004, and the BBC's "Forsyth Joins Impeach Blair Call" from the same date. One of the many reports on Adam Price's expulsion from Parliament is "Anti-Blair Jibe Leads to Commons Expulsion," the *Guardian,* March 17, 2005. Glenda Jackson's comments are found in "MPs Call on Blair to Go," the *Daily Mail,* May 8, 2005. The call for a Commons inquiry was broadly reported in articles such as "Blair Faces Iraq War Inquiry Move," BBC News, November 23, 2005, while the details of the motion and a list of its signers can be found at http://edmi.parliament.uk/EDMi/EDM Details.aspx?EDMID=29437&SESSION=875. General Sir Rose's comments were reported in "New Call to Impeach Blair Over Iraq" by Matthew Tempest, in the *Guardian,* January 9, 2006.

Chapter 3: Despots, Democrats and the Necessity of a Dissenting Opinion

The comment from James Mann, who drafted portions of two of the three articles of impeachment against Nixon that were approved by the Judiciary Committee, can be found in the Congressional Record and in Mann's extensive papers, which are kept among the University of South Carolina library's Modern Political Collections. Lord Bryce's "honest medicine" phrase is contained in his book *The American Commonwealth,* which was first published in London in three volumes in 1888. For a review of the Wisconsin Democratic Party's passage of its impeachment resolution, see Nichols, "State Parties Say: Impeach," *The Nation,* February 27, 2006. Details of the Zogby polls on impeachment can be reviewed at http://www.zogby.com, and activist David Swanson has written extensively and well on the subject of polling and impeachment at http://www.davidswanson.org. Good coverage of the San Francisco debate on impeachment was provided in a series of articles in the *San Francisco Chronicle,* including "S.F. supervisors set to debate call for impeachment of Bush, Cheney" by Phillip Matier and Andrew Ross (February 8, 2006) and "S.F. supervisors ask lawmakers to impeach Bush" by

Edward Epstein and Charlie Goodyear (March 1, 2006). The *San Francisco Bay Guardian* report on Pelosi's response was published as "The Case For Impeachment: It's Not Just for Radicals Anymore" by Steven T. Jones (January 25, 2006). The *San Francisco Bay Guardian* also addressed the debate in a February 1, 2006, editorial, "The Impeachment Issue." See also the May 13, 2006, *Chronicle* piece "A Democrat-Controlled House Wouldn't Impeach, Pelosi says," by Edward Epstein. MSNBC national affairs writer Tom Curry's March 17, 2006, review of Pelosi's response to impeachment appeared as "Who Does Impeachment/Censure Talk Benefit? Democrat Pelosi Sees Anti-Bush Acts as Diversion from Election Message" on MSNBC's website (www.msnbc.com).

For a sound history of the censure option, turn to the 1995 book *United States Senate Election, Expulsion, and Censure Cases, 1793–1990,* by Anne M. Butler and Wendy Wolff (available from the Government Printing Office). For more on Russ Feingold's censure fight, see several articles by the author in *The Nation,* including "Feingold Moves to Censure Bush" (March 13, 2006), "Censuring Censure" (March 17, 2006) and "Who Knew? GOP Says Feingold's Setting Dem Agenda" (March 17, 2006). The transcript of an April 11, 2006, interview of the author on the topic by radio journalist Scott Harris can be found on the Between the Lines website, http://www.btlonline.org, as "Democrats Fall for GOP Spin, Run Away from Feingold Censure Resolution." See also "Feingold's Censure Call a Distraction for His Party," an article by Christina Bellantoni that appeared March 20, 2006, in the *Washington Times,* and "A Senate Maverick Acts to Force an Issue: Democrat Feingold's Motion to Censure the President Roils Both Parties" by Shailagh Murray, which appeared March 15, 2006, in the *Washington Post.* For an assessment of Cheney's condemnation of Feingold, see "Censuring Censure" (*The Nation,* March 17, 2006), and the Associated Press report "Feingold Draws Little Support for Censure," published March 13, 2006.

Arianna Huffington's article "You Want to Discuss Impeachment? Give Me a Call on Nov. 8th" appeared February 9, 2006, on her excellent blog at http://www.huffingtonpost.com. Harold Meyerson's "Impeachment Imprudence" appeared March 8, 2006, in the *Washington Post*.

Former House minority whip Leslie Arends' dismissal of Nixon's impeachment as "a Democratic maneuver" was featured in a *Time* magazine article, "The Republicans' Moment of Truth," that appeared July 29, 1974, while former Senate minority leader Hugh Scott's comments appeared in a February 4, 1974, *Time* article, "Judging Nixon: The Impeachment Session." The records of partisan divisions in the House and Senate are available from the office of the House clerk and the Senate Historical Office. Good charts recounting those divisions are available for the Senate at http://www.senate.gov/pagelayout/history/one item_and_teasers/partydiv.htm and for the House at http://clerk .house.gov/histHigh/Congressional_History/partyDiv. html. For the best details on the 1998 election, see *The Almanac of American Politics, 2000* (Crown, 1999), by Michael Barone and Grant Ujifusa. Whitman's reference to "long dumb voices" can be found in the poem "Song of Myself."

Chapter 4: Rule-of-Law Republicanism: Conservative Crusaders Against the Imperial Presidency

Teddy Roosevelt's defense of dissent in wartime appeared in a May 7, 1918, column written for the *Kansas City Star*. Some of the best assessments of the efforts to hold John Tyler to account can be found in biographies of his chief congressional challenger, former president John Quincy Adams; one of the best of these is Paul C. Nagel's 1997 text *John Quincy Adams* (Knopf). See also the collection *Writings of John Quincy Adams*, which was last published in 1913 but can be found in major libraries. A very good article on Louis McFadden's attempt to impeach Herbert Hoover, "I Impeach . . . ," appeared December 26, 1932, in *Time* magazine. Jonathan Turley's "Senate Trials and Factional Disputes:

Impeachment as a Madisonian Device," 49 *Duke Law Journal* pp. 1–146 (1999), also provides useful information and insights on historic impeachments.

Murray Rothbard's article "Requiem for the Old Right," which appeared October 27, 1980, in the journal *Inquiry,* provides a good review of the career of George Harrison Bender and useful insights regarding Howard Buffett. Donald Johnson's article "Lessons from Korea" was written for the September 2000 edition of the *American Legion Magazine. To Chain the Dog of War* (University of Illinois Press, 1989), by Francis D. Wormuth and Edwin B. Firmage, is an outstanding resource, as is Louis Fisher's *Presidential War Power* (University Press of Kansas, 2004). James T. Patterson's *Mr. Republican* (Houghton Mifflin, 1972) is a useful biography of Robert Taft. Rothbard's "The Foreign Policy of the Old Right," which appeared in the *Journal of Libertarian Studies,* Vol. 2, No. 1 (1978), provided a great deal of background and insight, as did Ralph Raico's article "Harry S Truman: Advancing the Revolution," which first appeared in a 2001 book edited by John V. Denson, *Reassessing the Presidency* (Ludwig von Mises Institute, 2001). The same goes for Harry W. Berger's article "Senator Robert A. Taft Dissents from Military Escalation," which appeared in *Cold War Critics* (Quadrangle Books, 1971), a book edited by Thomas G. Paterson. My fellow Wisconsinite Stephen E. Ambrose's brilliant 1983 book, *Rise to Globalism* (Penguin), remains essential reading. Two biographies of Truman, Alonzo L. Hamby's *Man of the People* (Oxford University Press, 1995) and David McCullough's *Truman* (Simon and Schuster, 1992) were of particular value in assessing the president's attempt to take over the steel industry. The *New York Times* reported on Bender's impeachment proposal in its April 19, 1952, edition. A transcript of Dirksen's remarks regarding impeachment on the May 2, 1952, broadcast of CBS Radio's "Capitol Cloak Room" is available from the Dirksen Congressional Center in Pekin, Illinois. The citation for *Youngstown Sheet & Tube Co. v. Sawyer* is 343 U.S. 579 (1952), and a good review of the trial can be found in Maeva Marcus' *Truman and the Steel Seizure Case* (Columbia University

Press, 1977). William Henry Harbaugh's *Lawyer's Lawyer: The Life of John W. Davis* (Oxford University Press, 1978) is a reasonably sympathetic biography of a complex man.

A fine assessment of Lawrence Hogan's approach to the Watergate debate can be found in J. Anthony Lukas' *Nightmare* (Viking, 1976). For more on Hogan and other Republicans during the Watergate fight, see several detailed *Time* magazine articles from the era: "The Fateful Vote to Impeach" (August 5, 1974), "Republicans Revolt Over Watergate" (April 9, 1973) and "Republicans and Impeachment" (July 29, 1974). Representative Mark Kirk's floor speech on McClory was delivered February 8, 2001, and can be found on page H236 of the Congressional Record for that date.

Lloyd Grove's insightful article on Bob Barr, "Rep. Barr's New Quest: Impeachment," appeared in the *Washington Post* on February 10, 1998. See also Melinda Henneberger's May 9, 1998, *New York Times* piece, "The Georgia Republican Who Uses the I-Word." Barr's criticism of the PATRIOT Act was highlighted in many articles, including Nat Hentoff's "Terrorizing the Bill of Rights: 'Why Should We Care? It's Only the Constitution,' " which appeared November 9, 2001, in the *Village Voice.* For a more detailed read on Barr's sentiments, see his contribution to *It's a Free Country* (RDV Books, 2002), edited by Danny Goldberg, Robert Greenwald and Victor Goldberg. Consider also Barr's May 3, 2005, testimony before the Subcommittee on Crime, Terrorism and Homeland Security of the House Judiciary Committee. The former congressman's statement on the renewal of the PATRIOT Act was issued by Barr as a press release on March 2, 2006. For more on Republican opposition to the PATRIOT Act, see "Back to the Big Lie," an article by this author that appeared March 22, 2006, on *The Nation*'s website, http://www.thenation.com. An article on broader Republican opposition to the party's president, "Even Republicans Fear Bush," was published October 31, 2004, by *The Nation.* Pete McCloskey's piece "Nixon and Bush: Presidential Parallels" appeared July 17, 2005, in the *Sacramento Bee.* Ron Paul's December 27, 2005, article, "Domestic Surveillance and the PATRIOT Act," was circulated by the congressman and can be found on the web at http://www.house.gov/paul/tst/ tst2005/tst122605.htm. Bruce Fein's statement regarding the impeachment of George W. Bush was made December 19, 2005, on National Public Radio's The Diane Rehm Show, which is produced by WAMU in Washington, DC. Fein's March 31, 1997, *Insight on the News* article on President Clinton's "merchandising" of the White House was titled "White House fund-raisers could spell impeachment." "All the President's Power," by Thomas E. Woods Jr., was published January 30, 2006, by the *American Conservative.* Scott McConnell's "Kerry's the One" appeared November 8, 2004, in the same magazine. The breakouts for the American Research Group poll can be found at http://www .americanresearchgroup.com.

Chapter 5: When Once a Republic is Corrupted

Conversations with Robert Drinan, Ron Dellums and John Conyers over the years, many of which served as the basis for articles in *The Nation* and *The Progressive,* informed this section of the book. So, too, did conversations with Gore Vidal, which are a little like sitting down with one of the founders—although he would want me to point out that, while they may have been right about chaining the dogs of war, they were incredibly imperfect men.

The results of the polling on the Clinton impeachment process can be found at http://www.cnn.com/ALL POLITICS/stories/1998/. Michael Gartner's important article "How the Monica Story Played in Mid-America" appeared in the May/June 1999 edition of the *Columbia Journalism Review.* For more on the thinking of the founders with regard to the war powers issue, along with the thinking of successive American leaders quoted here, see the author's 2005 book, *Against the Beast* (Nation Books). Consider also Chalmers Johnson's *The Sorrows of Empire* (Metropolitan Books, 2004). In addition to the books of Madisonian and Hamiltonian writing referenced earlier, the collection *Letters of*

Pacificus and Helvidius on the Proclamation of Neutrality of 1793 (Scholars Facsimilies & Reprint, 1999), provided information and insight for this chapter. Lincoln's speeches in Congress can be found in a fine volume edited by Roy P. Basler, *Abraham Lincoln: His Speeches and Writings* (World Publishing Company, 1946). The "spot resolution" speech was delivered on December 22, 1847. Lincoln's letter to Herndon can be found in Basler's 1953 volume, *The Collected Works of Abraham Lincoln,* which was published by the Abraham Lincoln Association. Stanley Kutler's "There Will Absolutely Be No Dissension" appeared in the *Chicago Tribune* on March 18, 2003.

The extensive and essential papers of Robert Drinan are found in the Congressional Archives of the John J. Burns Library at Boston College. They contain documentation of and notes about the Nixon impeachment fight. Journalist Judith Coburn, who coanchored Pacifica Radio's live, gavel-to-gavel coverage of the Watergate hearings, penned a very useful November 22, 2005, article for TomDispatch.com that recalled Drinan's war-related article of impeachment "Worse Than Watergate? America Is Facing the Mother of All Constitutional Crises—and the Media Remains Silent." *Time*'s August 5, 1974, cover story, "The Fateful Vote to Impeach," provides good detail regarding Judiciary Committee consideration of the impeachment article Drinan offered.

Robert Byrd's "sleepwalking through history" speech was delivered February 12, 2003, on the Senate floor. A number of his other speeches from the same period cover similar themes and can be found in his book *Losing America* (W.W. Norton & Company, 2004). The Associated Press report on the Conyers/Bonifaz press conference was published February 14, 2003, as "Suit Challenges Bush War Authority." Bonifaz's very good book *Warrior King* (Nation Books, 2003) puts the basic case for impeachment of President Bush in historic context. Beth Hundsdorfer's report on Congressman Costello's call for impeachment hearings, "Costello Pushes Hearings on Cheney," appeared January 20, 2004, in the *Belleville News-Democrat.* The paperback edition of the author's book on Cheney, *The Rise and Rise of Richard B. Cheney* (The

New Press, 2005) examines many of the ethical, legal and political concerns raised by the vice president's actions. The official Senate biography of Agnew, found at http://www.senate.gov/artandhistory/history/
common/generic/VP_Spiro_Agnew.htm on the web, includes reference to Nixon's "impeachment insurance" line. The papers of former
congressman Hutchinson are found at the Gerald R. Ford Library, Ann
Arbor, Michigan. The *Washington Post's* "Vice President for Torture" editorial appeared October 26, 2005. Colonel Wilkerson's New America
Foundation appearance took place on October 19, 2005, and was
widely reported. Wilkerson later gave a number of important inter-
views. Among the many good articles on Wilkerson's assessment of the
administration is Dana Milbank's "Colonel Finally Saw Whites of Their
Eyes," which appeared October 20, 2005, in the *Washington Post.* I
would also recommend viewing his interview for the CNN documen-
tary *Dead Wrong,* an August 23, 2005, report of which, "Former aide:
Powell WMD speech 'lowest point in my life,'" can be found on
CNN.com at http://www.cnn.com/2005/WORLD/meast/08/19/
powelling/. The author's reports on Maurice Hinchey's challenges to
Cheney were published by *The Nation,* including "Dick Cheney Is Not
Above the Law," which appeared February 10, 2006, and "Libby: Bush,
Cheney Authorized Leaks," which appeared April 6, 2006. Congressman Cohen's "conspiracies are not born in the sunlight of direct observations" critique can be found in "The Fateful Vote to Impeach," the
Time magazine article of August 5, 1974. The *Los Angeles Times* editorial
"Bush's Third Term" appeared April 23, 2006. Senator Specter's "impeachment is a remedy" comment came during a January 15, 2006,
appearance on ABC's *This Week* program. The *Barron's* editorial "Unwarranted Executive Power: The Pursuit of Terrorism Does Not Authorize the President to Make Up New Laws" appeared December 26,
2005.

For details about the effort by John Conyers and others to examine
the implications of the Downing Street Memo, see *The Constitution in
Crisis,* which was authored by the Judiciary Committee Staff (Academy

Chicago Publishers, 2006) and "Conyers vs. The Post," John Nichols, *The Nation,* June 19, 2005. You can listen to a recording of the hearing the congressman organized on Pacifica Radio's website at http://www .pacifica.org/programs/20050616_Downing_Street_Memo_Hearings USSpecial_John_Conyers.html.

My December 20, 2005, article for *The Nation,* "Raising the Issue of Impeachment," details the congressman's resolutions. The After Downing Street coalition's website, http://www.afterdowningstreet .org, serves as a tremendous and constantly updated resource for infor- mation about the movement to hold the Bush administration to ac- count. The group Progressive Democrats of America maintains a very good website at http://www.pdamerica.org. Barbara Lee's article "We Must Stand Firm to Defend Principles Defining Our Nation" appeared February 17, 2006, in the *San Jose Mercury News.*

Afterword: What Then From Newfane?

Joseph Warren's "An Oration on the Second Anniversary of the Boston Massacre," which was delivered March 5, 1772, can be found in *Reading the American Past* Volume I, Third Edition (Bedford/St. Martin's, 2005), edited by Michael P. Johnson. The *Brattleboro Reformer* provided detailed coverage of the Newfane vote in a number of very good articles by re- porter Howard Weiss-Tisman, including "Newfane Resolution Seeks to Impeach President" (February 4, 2006) and "Impeach Bush Crusade Spreads Around County" (February 21, 2006). The author wrote about Dan DeWalt's revolt in a number of articles for *The Nation,* including "What, Then, From Newfane?" (March 7, 2006), "Vermont Towns Vote to Impeach" (March 8, 2006) and "Impeachment From Below: Legisla- tors Lobby Congress" (April 23, 2006). The article "Brattleboro Joins Impeachment Call" was distributed by the Associated Press on March 26, 2006. For details about the Brattleboro resolution visit http://www .ibrattleboro.com. Peter Freyne, the always outstanding political writer for the *Seven Days* newspaper of Burlington, Vermont, began writing about the efforts of Vermonters to make real the promise of Jefferson's Manual with a March 15, 2006, entry in his "Inside Track" column. He also wrote about the Democratic party's response in an April 12, 2006, piece, as did this writer in "Impeachment From Below: Legislators Lobby Congress," the April 23, 2006, article for *The Nation*. A good article on the Illinois effort by reporter John Huston, "Impeachment Sought: Yarbrough Pushes Resolution in General Assembly," appeared April 26, 2006, in the *Westchester Herald* newspaper.

Walt Whitman's "the sign of democracy" can be found in "Song of Myself."

ACKNOWLEDGMENTS

The idea for this book was first broached in an email to my editor at The New Press, Andy Hsiao, who embraced it immediately while adding nuance and focus to my notion that it was time to reclaim impeachment from the scared politicians and the tepid editorial writers who are more afraid of a "constitutional crisis" than they are of the high crimes and misdemeanors that undermine the republic. Andy is a brilliant editor and an even more brilliant comrade. I cherish my work with him and the rest of the crew at The New Press, including Melissa Richards, Maury Botton, Diane Wachtell, André Schiffrin, and copy editor extraordinaire Aja Shevelew.

My friend Bob McChesney, with whom I have worked for so many years on media-reform issues, cheered on this deviation from that important work—always recognizing the connection between reforming a pliant media and holding the executive branch to account. The same goes for Josh Silver, the exceptional executive director of Free Press, the nation's media-reform network. Katrina vanden Heuvel, the editor of *The Nation,* joined in the conversations about impeachment from the start, posing wise questions, pressing for more information, challenging, pushing, celebrating. It is a delight to work with her, as it is to work with Karen Rothmyer, Roane Carey, Judith Long, Marc Cooper, Ari Berman, Bill Greider, Betsy Reed, Mike Webb, Peter Rothberg and everyone else associated with America's oldest weekly journal of opinion. All hail my many great interns over the years, including Dean Powers, who fact-checked several of my articles on censure and impeachment.

Dave Zweifel, the editor of the *Capital Times,* a newspaper that has always been up for a good impeachment, remains the best in the business. I am honored to work with him, as I am with Phil Haslanger, Judy Ettenhofer, Linda Brazill and the rest of the defenders of the progressive vision of Robert M. La Follette who edit the paper in the tradition of the great dissenting journalist William T. Evjue.

My friend Matt Rothschild, the editor of *The Progressive,* has talked to me about impeachment just about every day for the past year. Ed Garvey has been in on the conversation from the start, as he always is. David Austin and Laura Dresser, Dana Maya and Courtney Johnson, Adam Benedetto, the ever-Green Ben Manski and OmaVic McMurray entertained every new factoid, story and enthusiasm, and frequently added some of their own. Barbara Lawton, John Stauber, Stanley Kutler, John Dean, Fred Wade, Tammy Baldwin, John Conyers and Maurice Hinchey gave of their time and wisdom.

Clarence Kailin, now well past ninety, is my friend and my inspiration, and he always puts big issues in the right perspective, as he certainly has in our discussions about war powers and presidential accountability; Clarence is active with Veterans for Peace, one of the first national groups to call for impeachment. Credit for inspiration goes as well to Buzz Davis, Bob Kimbrough and Dan DeWalt—champions of peace, justice and impeachment. Steve Cobble is a great friend and a great thinker about politics and democracy who helped to frame my thinking about this whole project, as did Tim Carpenter and David Swanson and others associated with the Censure Bush movement. A shout-out, as well, to my Old Right friends, who reminded me that true conservatives appreciate accountability just as much as true progressives.

Thanks to the baristas at Ancora Coffee Roasters on King Street in Madison. Thanks to the booksellers of the Rainbow Bookstore Collective in Madison, Borders West in Madison, Politics and Prose in Washington, Cody's in Berkeley, Odyssey Bookshop of western Massachusetts and all the shops that have given me a forum to try these ideas out in the context of tours for other books. Thanks to Fighting Bob Fest for putting me onstage with John Conyers. Thanks to Amy Goodman, Al Franken, Ed Schultz, Jay Marvin, Jon Wiener, Suzi Weissman, Lee

Rayburn and other progressive broadcasters for helping to spread the word; and thanks to Wisconsin Public Radio, WXXM 92.1 FM and WORT-FM for being the best broadcast forums in the country for honest dialogue. Thanks, finally, to the musicians who provided the soundtrack: Neil Young, whose "Let's Impeach the President" came out while I was writing the book, gets top billing this time. But Dan Bern, Dave Alvin, Steve Earle, Anti-Flag, Electric Six, Lou Reed, Patti Smith and Sean Michael Dargan were in heavy rotation. And, in deference to the British roots of impeachment, the Kinks, Killing Joke and Billy Bragg joined the mix, as did the transcendent Delroy Wilson, whose "Better Must Come" remains the best political song of all time.

This book, like all of my work, is a product of the dissenting spirit of my mother, Mary Nichols, and the egalitarian instinct of my father, Harrison Nichols. Whitman Genevieve Nichols Bottari asks all the right questions and is still cool enough to laugh at her own jokes. Mary Bottari makes everything happen. *The Genius of Impeachment* is dedicated to my great aunt Carolyn Fry, the most radical Daughter of the American Revolution I know, and my hero. She is the living embodiment of the progressive movement of the first years of the last century and remains ever at the ready to defend the republic against monarchs and mischief makers.

IMPEACHMENT FOR BEGINNERS: THE IMPEACHMENT PROCESS IN A NUTSHELL

1. The House Judiciary Committee deliberates over whether to initiate an impeachment inquiry.
2. The Judiciary Committee adopts a resolution seeking authority from the entire House of Representatives to conduct an inquiry. Before voting, the House debates and considers the resolution. Approval requires a majority vote.
3. The Judiciary Committee conducts an impeachment inquiry, possibly through public hearings. At the conclusion of the inquiry, articles of impeachment are prepared. They must be approved by a majority of the Committee.
4. The House of Representatives considers and debates the articles of impeachment. A majority vote of the entire House is required to pass each article. Once an article is approved, the President is, technically speaking, "impeached"—that is subject to trial in the Senate.
5. The Senate holds trial on the articles of impeachment approved by the House. The Senate sits as a jury while the Chief Justice of the Supreme Court presides over the trial.
6. At the conclusion of the trial, the Senate votes on whether to remove the President from office. A two-thirds vote by the Members present in the Senate is required for removal.
7. If the President is removed, the Vice-President assumes the Presidency under the chain of succession established by Amendment XXV to the U.S. Constitution.

Source: LII / Legal Information Institute, Cornell Law School. The LII maintains an outstanding online collection of impeachment-related historical documents, analyses and resources, which was developed during the Bill Clinton impeachment struggle but remains relevant and useful to this day. It can be found at http://www.law.cornell.edu/back ground/impeach/impeach.htm

IMPEACHMENT BY THE BOOK: AN EXECUTIVE EXCESS READING LIST

The Impeachment and Trial of Andrew Johnson
Michael Les Benedict
(W. W. Norton & Company; Reprint edition, 1999)

Historian Eric Foner hails this monograph, originally published in 1972, as "the definitive account of Andrew Johnson's impeachment and of the dramatic events that first put a president on trial before the Senate." That's an apt description by an able guide through the politics of reconstruction, which are, of course, completely linked to the impeachment of the 17th president. What is most appealing about Benedict's book for scholars of American impeachments, however, is the author's recognition of impeachment as an appropriate and necessary tool both for the removal of a miserable executive and for the advancement of the nation. Benedict provides a thorough history of the events surrounding the impeachment of Johnson—whose resistance to reconstruction cost the country an opportunity to renew the promise of the American experiment in the aftermath of the Civil War—and from it draws the conclusion that the attempt to remove the president should be seen as part of the "well-meaning efforts of conscientious Republicans to establish national security on the basis of equality before the law." Indeed, out of the whole sorry history of the failure of the United States to use the post-Civil War period to complete the mission of that war, Benedict argues, "Only one event has resisted this historical reversal—the impeachment and trial of President Andrew Johnson."

An interest in the era and Johnson's impeachment will lead readers also to Foner's brilliant *Reconstruction: America's Unfinished Revolution, 1863–1877* (Harper Perennial Modern Classics, 2002) and Eric L. McKitrick's thought-provoking Andrew Johnson and Reconstruction (Oxford University Press, USA, 1988).

The Wars of Watergate: The Last Crisis of Richard Nixon
Stanley Kutler
(W. W. Norton & Company; Reprint edition, 1992)

Kutler, the ablest historian of the modern presidency, places the end of Richard Nixon's tenure in proper political context. Reflections on Lyndon Johnson's imperial presidency, the abuses of power associated with the Vietnam War and Nixon's own cruelties and obsessions give readers the perspective they need to then join Kutler for an in-depth exploration of the Watergate crisis. The author does not casually employ the word "wars"; he recognizes Watergate as the fight that it was between a powerful executive and a Congress that was beginning to assert its Constitutional authority to check and balance the executive branch. Kutler's examination of House Judiciary Committee chairman Peter Rodino's handling of the impeachment process is as instructive as it is inspiring.

Further reading would, necessarily, include Times of London/BBC reporter Fred Emery's incredibly well-reported and well-written Watergate (Touchstone; Reprint edition, 1995) and Robert Scheer's excellent recent book Playing President: My Relationships with Nixon, Carter, Bush I, Reagan, and Clinton—And How They Did Not Prepare Me for George W. Bush (Akashic Books; Paperback, 2006).

The Federal Impeachment Process:
A Constitutional and Historical Analysis
Michael J. Gerhardt
(University Of Chicago Press; 2nd edition, 2000)

Though this is a general history, the second edition contains the best reflection on the impeachment of Bill Clinton, in which Gerhardt was something of a player—as a well-regarded commentator and expert witness on the Constitutional issues that were raised. Gerhardt understands impeachment as a political process, designed and best used to address political crimes and challenges. He examines the Clinton impeachment from this perspective and comes to the conclusion that the president's trial and acquittal fit rather more neatly than some imagine into the long arc of impeachment history.

Two additional perspectives, of a somewhat more incendiary character—depending on the politics of the reader—are offered by Bob Barr's The Meaning of Is: The Squandered Impeachment and Wasted Legacy of William Jefferson Clinton (Stroud & Hall, 2004) and Washington Post reporter Peter Baker's *The Breach: Inside the Impeachment and Trial of William Jefferson Clinton* (Scribner, 2000).

Warrior King: The Case for Impeaching George Bush
John Bonifaz
(Nation Books, 2003)

Shamefully overlooked at the time of its publication, largely because potential readers were convinced that George W. Bush would be "dealt with" in the 2004 election, Bonifaz's book makes the case that the president violated the Constitution when he led the United States into the Iraq quagmire without a Congressional declaration of war and—as history has confirmed for all but the most fervent apologists—without telling the truth to Congress or the American people. Bush haters will love this book, while Bush defenders will hate it. Both of these takes are wrong. Bonifaz, a lawyer and MacArthur Foundation "genius grant" re-

cipient, has a rich record of challenging wrongdoing by leaders and legislators of both parties. Warrior King's strength is as an argument for
preventing any president—Republican or Democrat, conservative or
liberal, incompetent or able—from tossing aside the Constitution in
order to wage a war of whim.

A companion volume, written in a different time about a different
president but dealing with the same problem is *Unquestioning Obedience
to the President: The ACLU Case Against the Legality of the War in Vietnam*,
written more than three decades ago by Leon Friedman and Burt
Neuborne (W.W. Norton & Company, 1972). U.S. Representative John
Conyers, the ranking Democrat on the House Judiciary Committee,
wrote the introduction to Bonifaz's book. He is, as well, responsible for
the release of *The Constitution in Crisis: The Downing Street Minutes and
Deception, Manipulation, Torture, Retributions and Cover-ups in the Iraq War*
(Academy Chicago Publishers, 2006), the staff report on Bush White
House wrongdoing that is referenced frequently in Chapter 5 of this
book.

The Case for Impeachment: The Legal Argument for
Removing President George W. Bush from Office
Dave Lindorff and Barbara Olshansky
(Thomas Dunne Books, 2006)

Thorough in detail and analysis, this book by Lindorff, a veteran journalist, and Olshansky, who directs litigation for the Center for Constitutional Rights, lays the groundwork for the impeachment of President
George W. Bush for lying to the American people about the Iraq war, illegally spying on U.S. citizens, seizing undue executive power, and
sending people to be tortured overseas. It's a useful text not merely for
its review of the administration's wrongdoing, but also for the able manner in which it explains both the legal ramifications of that wrongdoing
and the available remedies. Olshansky and others with the Center for
Constitutional Rights have been in the forefront of the legal fight to

hold the Bush administration for authorizing the indefinite incarceration of "enemy combatants"—even when they are American citizens—without charge or access to legal representation at the Guantánamo Bay Naval Base and elsewhere. This book is especially strong in its assessment of the Constitutional concerns raised by that tactic.

The Center has produced a useful text, *Articles of Impeachment Against George W. Bush* (Melville House, 2006), which provides a concise outline of specific articles of impeachment that might be brought against the president and members of his administration. Another book that suggests articles of impeachment against Bush is University of Illinois law professor Francis Anthony Boyle's *Destroying World Order: U.S. Imperialism in the Middle East Before and After September 11th* (Clarity Press, 2004).

IMPEACHMENT IN THE HERE AND NOW:
A RESOURCE GUIDE

AfterDowningStreet.org
Impeachment Resource Center

The message is blunt: "Impeach Bush and Cheney Now!" Those who share the sentiment will find a wealth of resources at AfterDowning-Street's constantly-updated website, http://www.afterdowningstreet .org/resourcecenter, which has become a go-to site for activists seeking the impeachment of President Bush and Vice President Cheney. Founded in 2005 by anti-war activists seeking to raise awareness of British documents that confirmed the Bush-Cheney administration had deceived the U.S. Congress, the American people and international allies to make the "case" for invading Iraq, the AfterDowningStreet coalition has become a prime player in the push for impeachment. The groups' website tracks congressional support for the resolutions sponsored by U.S. Representative John Conyers to censure Bush and Cheney and to explore whether the president and vice president should be impeached. It highlights national and local organizing on the issue. And it provides sample resolutions supporting impeachment, along with lists of city councils, political groups and organizations that have passed them. The site also features many links to other national and local groups working on these issues.

ImpeachPAC

Founded by activists associated with the popular website http://www
.democrats.com, ImpeachPAC is a political action committee that raises
money with the purpose of "[electing] Democratic candidates for Congress who support the immediate and simultaneous impeachment of
George Bush and Dick Cheney for their Iraq War lies." Bob Fertik, the
founder and president of ImpeachPAC, developed one of the first pro-
impeachment initiatives, ImpeachCentral.com http://ImpeachCentral
.com, in 2003 to organize grassroots support for impeachment of the
president and vice president. Allied with the AfterDowningStreet Coalition, ImpeachPAC endorses pro-impeachment congressional candidates and used the web to raise money to support them. It also promotes
the passage of local-government resolutions urging the impeachment of
Bush and Cheney, and provides links from its www.impeachpac.org
website to many useful tools for grassroots activists, including A Guide to
the Impeachment of George W. Bush and Richard Cheney, written by
Phil Burk, Richard Mathews and Sophie de Vries.

American Civil Liberties Union

The nation's premier civil liberties defense organization has taken the
lead in challenging the Bush administration's warrantless wiretapping of
the telephone calls of Americans, which the ACLU argues are in violation of the Fourth Amendment and other Constitutional protections
guaranteed to Americans. After it was revealed that President Bush had
authorized the National Security Agency to spy on Americans without
following legal requirements for such initiatives, the ACLU filed a law-
suit against the NSA on Jan. 17, 2006. The organization has also coordinated filings across the nation with state public service commissions,
demanding that regulators investigate any illegal spying by phone companies that have provided records to the NSA.

"President Bush may believe he can authorize spying on Americans without judicial or Congressional approval, but this program is illegal and we intend to put a stop to it," says ACLU Executive Director Anthony D. Romero. "The current surveillance of Americans is a chilling assertion of presidential power that has not been seen since the days of Richard Nixon." The ACLU has publicized its challenge to Bush with an advertising campaign that makes comparisons to Nixon-era wrongdoing. Next to a photo of Nixon, the advertisements declare: "He lied to the American people and broke the law." Next to a photo of a Bush is the line: "So did he." The ads ask: "What should we do when the U.S. President lies to us and breaks the law?" They then call on Congress to "renew its bipartisan commitment to our Constitutional system of checks and balances."

The ACLU maintains an excellent website at http://www.aclu.org and can also be contacted at: ACLU, 125 Broad Street, 18th Floor, New York, NY 10004. It maintains chapters across the country.

The Center for Constitutional Rights

Declaring that "Congress must go beyond censure and consider impeachment," the Center for Constitutional Rights has taken a lead in pushing for specific articles of impeachment against Bush. "Recent calls for a censure resolution show that some senators finally realize that President Bush is out of control," CCR argues. "But a censure resolution will not: Remove a single wiretap from American phones; End the Iraq War; Halt U.S. Torture; or stop President Bush's reckless abuse of power." CCR, which was founded in 1966 by lawyers who had earned their spurs in the civil rights era has a long history of challenging executive excess and illegality. It's been organizing town hall meetings on impeachment and related issues, details of which can be obtained on the web at http://www.ccr-ny.org, where it is also possible to find recommended articles of impeachment. The group can be contacted by regular mail at Center for Constitutional Rights, 666 Broadway, 7th Floor, New York, NY 10012.

National Lawyers Guild

The National Lawyers Guild was one of the first groups, along with Veterans for Peace, to start talking about impeaching members of the Bush administration. The memorandum on the issue developed in 2003 by the group's San Francisco Bay Area Chapter and the articles of impeachment developed by the organization are detailed and well thought. They're available on the group's website at http://www .nlg.org, or from its headquarters at National Lawyers Guild, National Office, 132 Nassau Street, Ste. 922, New York NY 10038. Of special interest are the group's statements on the prospect that the neglect of Hurricane Katrina victims by administration officials might well qualify as an impeachable offense.

Vote to Impeach

The Vote to Impeach movement asks Americans to declare: "I want my representative in the U.S. House of Representatives to vote to impeach President George W. Bush, Vice President Richard B. Cheney, Secretary of State Condoleezza Rice, Secretary of Defense Donald H. Rumsfeld, and Attorney General Alberto Gonzales for high crimes and misdemeanors, and to have the case prosecuted and tried in the U.S. Senate." It has developed articles of impeachment for members of the Bush administration, which can be reviewed at its website—http://www .impeachbush.org—or by writing VoteToImpeach, c/o 5505 Connecticut Ave. NW, # 299 Washington, DC 20015. Former Attorney General Ramsey Clark, whose consistent critique of U.S. foreign policy has made him a subject of controversy is a key supporter of this group, which shares Clark's concern about violations of international law. "Impeachment is essential to the integrity of constitutional government," says Clark. "It is the most urgent duty of the American people. We have the power to cause impeachment, if we have the will."

Impeach for Peace

The Minnesota-based group, Impeach for Peace, does a great job of combining on-the-ground activism with web-based initiatives. Their http://www.impeachforpeace.org website has loads of links and a great set of responses to arguments against impeachment. For instance: To the line, "It hurts the democracy to go through a presidential impeachment," the Impeach for Peace folks respond, "Holding government officials accountable for their actions strengthens our democracy. Letting lawlessness stand weakens it." To the question, "But won't we then get President Cheney?" they reply, "Initiating the impeachment process would lead to an investigation that would implicate lots of people in the Bush administration who are guilty of committing crimes, including Cheney."

Impeach Bush Yardsigns Campaign

One of the most remarkable grassroots pro-impeachment campaigns in the country began in Ann Arbor, Michigan, where activists began distributing "Impeach Bush" yardsigns last year. Driving through the city, it's impossible to miss the red, white and blue signs. They're everywhere. And the movement has spread to other Michigan cities, as well. The campaign operates off a website, http://www.impeachbushyardsigns .org, which also includes a fine collection of articles and resolutions and, of course, pictures of the signs in the yards of supporters. The site explains, "We are a group of people in Ann Arbor, Michigan, who are tired of George Bush getting away with high crimes and misdemeanors that are more than enough to justify impeachment. And conviction. Help us move impeachment further into mainstream debate. Put a sign in your front yard. Get a few for your friends. It feels good."

INDEX